I Don't Do Vanilla

I DON'T DO VANILLA

Jodi Barrett

I Don't Do Vanilla
Barrett, Jodi

ISBN 978-1-7380094-0-4 (paperback)
ISBN 978-1-7380094-1-1 (ebook)

Edited by Katie Beaton, Veneration
Cover design by Publish and Promote
Book Production by Publish and Promote
Cover photo by Cara Barschel
Interior layout and design by Davor Nikolic

Printed and bound in Canada

Disclaimer: This memoir is written from the author's own memories and perspective, without any intention of offending anyone.

DEDICATION

I wrote this book to heal, to share, and to grow.

I dedicate this book to my mom, my dad, my children (Connor, Mira, and Ava), and my QOP (Quality-Only People) who held my hand and lifted me up when I felt I could no longer get back up.

To my mom and dad: I know you doubted my idea at the start because you were scared of the road I would have ahead of me. Thank you for never giving up on me and becoming my biggest supporters. I believe it is my tenacity, my grit, and my endless love for the challenges I have faced and walked through that gives me the strength to go on.

To my children: Whether or not you ever read this, or even if you read it and potentially don't understand, may one day you understand the love I carry within for each of you, and that if I had known better in some of life's moments, I would have done better. Our society sees the woman give up so much of herself for her children, and then when we don't, we are frowned upon. I struggled with this. I feel the story I will share will hopefully shed some light on how you can accomplish your dreams in the midst of chaos. I think we must share and grow and know that we all need goals and a zest for life.

To my friends: You know who you are, the ones who talked me off the ledge so many times, who had my back and reminded me that they believed in me in the moments I found doubt within myself. I love you all so much. I hope when you read this, you will laugh, you will cry, and you will simply remember to LIVE.

Absorb what is useful, discard what is useless and add what is specifically your own.

—Bruce Lee

CONTENTS

PREFACE

Do you ever wonder why in a world where we know our time is limited, we act as if we have a lifetime to live? I thought about this a lot in the last ten years. I sat with it, how we feel miserable, always rushed, doing jobs we hate while never pausing long enough to watch the beauty of a sunrise or a sunset because we are tired or there's simply not enough time to pause.

Years ago, I had a rebirth. I saw life through what felt like the eyes of a child. I was so uncertain of so many things, but I was certain of two things: Training kept me sane within my chaos, and death was promised to us all. I do not mean to be morbid, but I will no longer walk through life hating myself and missing out on experiences. I will go after my biggest dreams because when the day comes, and it I will, I can take my last breath and know that I lived my life to the fullest.

I have often been asked, "If you could change your path to avoid the pain and the challenges, would you?" I am always quick to answer, "No." Every scar I possess has built me. On my hardest days being alone, I remind myself that I'd rather walk through life as a single female than lie beside another human and feel alone.

Why *I Don't Do Vanilla*? I've always preferred chocolate; I am referring to chocolate chips, chocolate brownies, and chocolate men. Okay, kind of funny, but did you think this whole book was going to be serious? I think in this life, we need to laugh, smile, and never take ourselves that seriously. At one point, I was never going to date White men again, but that is yet to be determined. More specifically, I don't do vanilla, meaning I don't do things the way most people do. I dream big and strive to push where I believe I want to go.

You may be wondering, *Why did a stay-at-home mom of eleven years choose to leave her family unit to launch a business in the fitness industry??* Why would I do that? Because I don't do vanilla. Well, not anymore! It sounds cheesy, but I have a knowing within my soul that it is my purpose for being here. I have also realized that even when you know your purpose, you are going to have to walk through some very hard moments. I am not a stranger to hard moments; maybe that is why I am resilient, and maybe that is why this is my path.

First of all, I did not just wake up and decide to become an entrepreneur. It was a process. This memoir is my story about how my eleven years of staying in one lane changed so drastically. It is a story of how I do and see things differently, and why this big heart has such a big purpose!

The obvious place to start is my childhood, as it taught me many things about life, such as grit, resilience, adversity, pain, love, and perspective. Then came my marriage, my children, and then my failed marriage. All of these I believe were lessons so I could get here.

I want to tell you that this life can be so messy, so crazy, and so fucking scary at times, but it is also so worth it if you are ready to just embrace it all. Learn to experience life instead of reacting to it. I used to be so good at pushing my feelings deep down, but once I started to learn, to listen, and to keep learning, I have since gotten to do things in the past ten years that I could have never imagined previously. I get to write my story every day. When I completed my first published chapter in a previous book, my son asked how I could write about my story when I had so many chapters of life yet to live. He was right, but taking time now to write my story feels like a new start, yet again.

As I got ready to write my story, I was reminded that sometimes, one has to dip their toes into the water before taking the plunge. I may be seen as a plunge-right-in girl, but truthfully, I double-dip my toes all the time. These are the ups and downs, the completely messed-up moments that rocked my world and ultimately shifted my entire story.

Our past does not define us, but it is part of us. To find our strength, we must recognize that weakness needs to be present. If there are no moments of weakness, we will never be able to show our strengths.

CHAPTER 1:

FAITH

My Marriage

You see, I did not wish or dream of getting married and having children. I wanted a career; I wanted to be able to take care of myself, build my future, and then if life wanted to lead me to marriage and children, I would embrace it—but it wasn't part of my plan. I have learned that sometimes the plan gets changed, and life never goes as planned!

The year I graduated from university, I got married three months later! In moments, I went from striving to be an independent young woman to someone who now wanted a perfect family! I don't know how it happened, how I got so off course with my goals and dreams, but I did, and before I knew it, I had a two-year-old, and I was so excited when I found out we were pregnant again. After waiting to get my gallbladder removed, we were given the go-ahead to try for number two. My perfect family was happening, and I was fully embracing this new way, this new idea. The plan had shifted drastically, and events in my life would soon unexpectedly pull me under a current hard and fast, leaving me grappling to pull myself back to the surface.

My Perfect Family Life

I had decided I could make our life perfect, and having two children was part of the idea I had in my mind. The day we headed to our ultrasound, we were so excited, and within moments, our excitement was quickly replaced with fear. This lovely little human inside me had fluid in their abdomen cavity, and so much fluid in their chest cavity that it had pushed their heart to the side. Now, it may have been only millimetres, but when you hear the word "pushed," you visualize the heart pressed up against the furthest part. I don't remember much from the elevator ride back to the car, but I remember feeling like I couldn't hear. You know when you get bad news, and you feel like you are having an out-of-body experience, and you can't speak, and your whole body feels numb?! My heart was racing, but I was thinking, *Breathe, Jodi. This little person needs you to breathe.*

This was the beginning of a journey where I would fight for this little person, who we found out through amniocentesis was my baby girl.

Fast forward: We discovered the fluid was miraculously dissipating, hence our daughter's name is Mira, as she was our miracle, our gift, our fighter. She was diagnosed before birth with a genetic disorder that could have been a spectrum of things. You know when you prefer life to tell you black or white, go or stop, up or down? Well, this life situation handed us gray. We knew having her could be a walk in the park or it could be a challenge. We didn't know what to expect. I took the sign that all fluid had dissipated as a sign that all would be okay.

As the delivery got closer, I was still scared. I sometimes talked to her and told her I wished for her to stay inside me where I could keep her safe. Along with feeling scared and hormonal, I started to feel angry toward my partner, whom had been my world. I was angry that he could go out golfing, to work functions, and play in a band on weekends, while I could never leave as I was very, very pregnant and running after a toddler. I loved being a mom, but I was sensing a disconnect from my husband for the first time. I don't even know if I realized it then as much as I did years later.

On September 26th, 2002, I delivered the cutest little baby girl with a button nose. We took her home after only twenty-six hours. As I had already had a baby before, I guess they thought I knew what I was doing. Not long after getting Mira home, she became colicky—or so we thought, until the colic was replaced with a failure to thrive. We were so sure she was okay. Looking back at the pictures, I have often scolded myself for not seeing what was going on, as the pictures show a very sick little girl.

Mira's first Christmas was spent in the hospital. We even got a tree for the hospital, and on Christmas, our moms pitched in to stay with her so we could find some normalcy with our two-year-old.

After Christmas, they released her, saying she was better. I was beginning to think they just didn't know. January took us to Saskatoon hospital where they still didn't know. They put us in the same room as a child who had a violent flu. I believe this moment began my journey of unlocking my voice because

I recognized that I had to become a voice for my baby. My husband and I took her out of the hospital as being in close quarters with a potential virus was not the best idea. We would connect with the doctor and come up with another plan.

We ended up admitted back to the hospital in Regina in February, and they had no idea either. I remember her pediatrician saying, "Jodi, I just lay awake at night stressing that I don't know what to do!" I thought, *Are you fucking kidding me? At least be professional and keep the worry to yourself.* I needed someone to be strong and tell me it was going to be okay, yet here I was having to be strong for a doctor. Things were not changing. My little baby, who was five months old, still looked like a newborn. Something had to change quickly. I decided I had to be the strong one.

On February 14th, 2003, I took an air ambulance with Mira to Stollery Children's Hospital in Edmonton. They had exhausted all options in Regina, and so we needed to go. That day, my dad showed up with flowers for me and his granddaughter. I will never forget the gesture, as he knew we were flying out, but I love flowers, and it was his way of doing what he could. Mira and I got into the ambulance and I thought about how I had previously vowed never to get on a plane after my honeymoon, as turbulence terrified me. Now, I stepped out onto the tarmac to the tiniest plane, with one nurse and one pilot. When you love someone, you don't bat an eye while doing something for them that scares you. She was my ride or die, and I would put all my fears away to find a way to help her get better. From that moment forward, I was no longer the same person. I would no longer sit back and watch as people tried to solve issues for my daughter. I would learn to be a fighter right alongside my daughter.

I didn't know it, but I was slowly retreating from all my friends, and I wasn't eating. When my mom came, she made me go shopping so my clothes would fit. Mira wasn't gaining weight, and I was losing weight drastically. I had no desire to eat, and eating became simply a moment just to put food in so I would have some energy to do what I needed. We would weigh Mira every day, and I watched as she gained a little and then lost a little. We did so many cystic fibrosis tests that I eventually learned how to watch the numbers on the machines so I would know the result before they even told me.

I journaled every day, mostly about how much Mira weighed and how I missed my family. I would journal about how long she slept too. It was anything and nothing of importance, just something for my well-being, as I was in such a lonely space. I remember reading back through the writings and the day I finally wrote to God. I had been so angry that I had chosen to believe there was no God. Now, whatever your faith, I believe in a higher power. Sometimes, I simply think *higher power*, and sometimes I call this higher power *God*.

The point being that I was angry for a while, like when I discovered something wasn't right at that first ultrasound. But during my time in Edmonton, I finally realized I needed God. I needed a higher power to talk to and help me make sense of it all. I needed someone present with me to be part of my team. I was beginning to feel very disconnected from my husband, family, and friends. I felt separated and was searching for oneness within, with someone.

Day nineteen: Tuesday, March 4th, 2003
Weight: 11 lb. 6.7 oz.
Height: 58.55 cm (from 56.2 cm on February 14th)

Well, the day "ticketed" by, and still they say, "Sorry, no results." I feel the pressure as if I'm made of concrete and have been put under a high-pressure system. I am starting to crack. I don't know if I can take much more—God, find me the strength to go on. I'm falling apart on the inside, and I wonder if it is starting to show through. I don't care to eat. I could yell at the drop of a hat. I want to take Mira home to her family. It's been so hard, and it's getting harder. I know things could be worse, but this is our worst right now. Deep breath, close your eyes, and say a small prayer to God that tomorrow will be a day of answers.

I often wonder if these were the breaking down moments or the building up moments. Only later in life did I realize they were both, as you cannot build up until you break down.

When my husband was out with my son, we had a meeting with a team of experts to make a plan. They had no idea but had a big fancy test they could try, although it would take time to set it up. I remember Dr. Jones, a gastroenterologist, saying, "It's time to shit or get off the pot!" I couldn't have agreed more; it was time to find a solution. As part of that solution, they decided we needed to go home. Dr. Sam, who was the main doctor on Mira's case, came to me one day and said, "You need to go home, Jodi. We will figure it out and bring you back, but you need to go home and rest." They were now not only concerned about my daughter but worried about me too.

So I flew back home with my mom and my little girl so she could get a Total Parenteral Nutrition (TPN) line put in. I would learn to hook her up and make sure she was getting nutrition to not only grow but to develop.

I was so happy to be home, but with no diagnosis, I was frustrated. I went to the hospital, where they put in a central line, and I learned how to clean it and set it up. I was petrified she would get an infection, as when she was in Edmonton, she at one point went septic. I was now going to be in charge of her central line, as well as being in charge of a two-year-old and a household. My husband did not learn, and truthfully, I don't think I would have let him. However, I wish he had insisted on learning so that we could have both carried the responsibility. Looking back, I understand the importance of partnership, and I see that we were shifting away from this.

April, May, and some of June, Mira was at home with her TPN. I would hook up the machine, and it would beep occlusion, meaning there was an error on the machine or a bend in the tubing. Normal wasn't feeling very normal, and I was searching to find a way back to what I wanted normal to be. I was diligently searching case studies that showed anything and everything about what this might be. In June, we had to fly back out to Edmonton for the big, fancy test. I flew out alone with a car seat, a bag of clothes, and a research study that I'd found. When they did the test, it didn't work. I looked at Dr. Sam and said, "Can we please do a barium swallow test?" He said, "Well, that likely won't work, but to appease you, we will do it." Guess what? It was the one test that was in the research I had found that had diagnosed four Asian babies with intestinal lymphangiectasia, also called Waldmann's disease.

Her diagnosis after the barium swallow test? Intestinal lymphangiectasia. Her gastroenterologist later said to me that the barium swallow test should have been the first test done. Hindsight can be a bitch sometimes.

I didn't care, as we finally knew. They booked our nine-month-old for exploratory surgery to see if they could remove the damaged intestine. They said the surgery could take a while, if they could remove it. They showed up outside the hospital room quite quickly. I remember seeing them at the door and all I could think was that they were too fast to remove anything.

I immediately swallowed that hard lump in my throat and kept the tears inside as they told me that the area affected was too scattered throughout. Again, I experienced that feeling of being outside my body, just watching a story unfold. Truthfully, as I write this, I know I flew out there by myself for the test and the surgery. I felt so alone, but if you ask my ex, maybe he was there for the test. I cannot remember him there for the test. I just remember being alone. I find it interesting how we remember things, and how our feelings reflect how we see and perceive things.

When we returned home, our pediatrician told me I should meet up with a mom of an eight-year-old who had been on TPN since they were a baby. I agreed to meet her, as often I think that if it makes someone else feel better, I will go through with it. I did say, "I will do it to appease you, but I know Mira will not be on TPN forever because in my research, babies who had way worse results than her have gotten off TPN."

After my research on my very large, archaic computer, I always knew and was so confident that she wouldn't need to be on TPN forever. Three days before her first birthday, she had surgery to remove the line. I am not saying I am smarter than doctors, but I believe mothers have an intuition about our children. It is a sense, a knowing. I actually believe that if we listen, we can figure out a lot about this life. I could write a whole book on the first year with Mira, but maybe another time. I wanted to share how going through the experience taught me to have faith again. I learned to stand up for the ones who cannot use their voices. I was also shown how parts of my marriage were starting to fail, or maybe it uncovered areas that were flawed. Most marriages don't have one big moment where it goes wrong but rather lots of little ones that are left unaddressed. There were beginning to be moments of disconnect that I covered up with life and focusing on my children.

Getting Back to Normal

After a year of forever feeling worried and scared, life got back to our new normal, and I threw myself into being a mom. We had made the decision after Mira was so sick that if we could afford for me to stay home, I would officially be a stay-at-home mom. I remember thinking how great it was for my children that I'd always be able to go to all their activities and be there when they got home from school. I was going to crush being a mom. I planned out daily activities for my kids. As I also had a three-year-old, we would have craft time, dance time, and well, messy fun. I didn't realize it then, but I had fallen in love with my children. I know it sounds odd, but I lived and breathed for them.

Whenever I felt disconnected with my husband, I would focus more on my kids. Things were not bad with my husband at the time, but we were allowing our children to consume and alter our world. Instead of inviting them into our world, we began creating a different world. I will tell this to any of my friends who are expecting babies, "Make them a part of your world, so you don't lose yourself or your relationship."

In 2005, our family grew to five when I had Ava. She was a beautiful, smiley, little baby. I felt like life was back on track. I had my three children, and my husband came home one day to tell me he'd found the perfect house for our perfect family. I worked so hard on perfection; I would navigate from a place of fear of not being perfect. So, three children: one-month-old, three-year-old, and five-year-old. I began packing up to move us to our new home. It was in a suburb of Regina, so I was going to be a suburban mom. I took my role very seriously.

I scheduled Mondays for cleaning and laundry. My house was immaculate, not a toy to be found on the floor if we had company, and the children were in bed on time every night but with mini snack bowls first. I would get everyone ready and tucked in, and dad would swoop in and give goodnight kisses. He thought I was perfect. So when he needed to go on a trip to Mexico when Ava was three-months-old, and with a new home and a three- and five-year-old to care for too, I was supportive. I said, "Go, it's your job." And I was great at mine.

I was so perfect that I would scrape snow off the roof of the house after a storm while I let him unwind from his busy day, watching poker with a plate I made from supper. When I'd ask if he would join me and the kids for a walk, I would understand if he declined because he was tired from work and just needed time. This was my role, my job; I was the stay-at-home mom, so the house and the children were my job. Little did I realize, I was becoming more and more disconnected from him and from myself.

I remember we got invited to a white party. I was so excited. I got a dress and was ready to be around adults, but later, my husband just really didn't want to go. I didn't say anything about how disappointed I was, but I cried. I cried because I just wanted a night out, a night to not be a mom, but then I scolded myself because he was providing for us. Why should I raise my opinion or voice when he had bought us this house and took financial care of us? I was getting really good at pushing my feelings down like they didn't matter. The younger version of me was unsure what a marriage looked like, so I think I was navigating it the best I could.

As I started to think about what I wanted, I remember going out for my cousin's birthday one night at Earls. The kids were old enough to be at home. I had put dinner in the oven so it would be done when my husband arrived home. It was rare for me to go out, and I got a call from him as I was already driving home. He said, "The kids are starving, and where is dinner?" I was pissed. If they didn't want to wait, the kids were capable of opening a can of Alpha-getti, and well, I was on my way home.

I always had to run the ship, and I would tie myself up in knots trying to make sure everyone else was getting taken care of. I used my voice that day, and while it was refreshing for me to do so, it also reminded me of how boxed in I had felt, and how I had lost the ability for my own family to understand I was worthy of self-care. I was doing too much for everyone, and the more I did, the more they expected. I had given them permission to treat me as if I was not worth moments for myself. I think this was one of the hardest things. I should have navigated better. I should have known better, but you don't know until you know, and then you do better.

The Gym Reflection

The true moment I knew I had to fess up to my shit was that famous day at the gym. Why famous? I laugh because I have written about it many times as I have told my story for my business. I would go to the gym three to four times a week for an hour and a half to two hours.

Prior to doing weight training when the kids were little, I would get up and go swimming at 5:45 a.m. to sneak in some me time, or was it I was sneaking in some masking time? I don't know if I like the term masking, but I believe training saved me as it allowed me a break to continually build up who I was.

One day, I was sitting on the bench and staring at my reflection in the mirror. Who did I see? What did I see? I was physically strong, and I was disciplined.

Until that moment in the gym. The moment when I thought I was broken, but life was really building me for my moment of being brave. The moment to find the courage to use my voice again. That day, staring back at myself, I didn't lift a thing. I got up, grabbed my gym bag, and went for a walk. I stood on a bridge and looked out at the water as tears streamed down my face. This was the moment that I finally broke free. I allowed myself to become aware of it all: how I felt and how I had let things get so bad. The tears represented the possibility to free my soul and to find me again.

I knew I had to leave my marriage. It had been a year of pretending I was okay and trying to be this perfect person, but I just wanted to be me. Who the hell was I? And how would I navigate this when my decision would rock four other lives? What right did I have to love myself enough to be worthy of being happy? Was I worth it? These questions spun around in my head. Should one stay for financial reasons when they are not happy? Should one stay if they feel alone in the relationship?

I had watched others stay for many different reasons, and I kept coming back to the belief that everyone is worthy of love and happiness. Deep down, I knew I was worthy of the life I wanted. I wanted my husband to be loved as a husband should be, but I wasn't that person anymore. I could not be someone I was not anymore. I didn't know at the time that it would be so hard, and I am glad for that because sometimes I think it is best to just start walking through hell and hope to come to the other side.

We did the counseling, though I knew deep down I was just going through the motions. My husband felt blindsided and rightfully so, I thought, because I was always trying to just make everyone happy and not voice my opinion. And here I found I was doing it again because I had agreed with him, until one day, we talked and I said, "If we are so connected, how come you didn't notice how sad and disconnected I was?" I was learning that marriage was a partnership. I used to think of it as roles. His role and mine, but not a partnership, and it sure as hell wasn't supposed to look perfect. At one of our counseling sessions, the counselor asked me what it was like to be placed on the perfect podium. I cried, as I was exhausted, alone, and I didn't want to be freaking perfect anymore.

Over the next five to six years of my life, I got dragged through the mud, and I went from living a seemingly perfect life to feeling confused to feeling that I was perfectly a piece of shit. My life felt shattered when we told our kids we were separating. This is the moment I use to gauge all my hard moments. If something scares me or unnerves me, I think of this moment. I think about how I survived that, so anything else is a walk in the park. This was the journey of how my life evolved, how I refused to settle, and how I decided that I mattered. This is my story and my perspective on how training brought me to a place of bravery to navigate and grow myself and my business.

CHAPTER 2:

GRIT

Sharing the News

Telling people we were separating was one of the strangest experiences ever. I had to comfort people who cried while saying, "Not you guys. If you guys can't make it, no one can." Oh my God, I learned very quickly what people thought and who were my true friends. My dad was disgusted with me, and that was a hard one. I think he thought I had royally fucked things up. People see the big house, the trips, the things we could buy, and they can't understand why I would walk away from that. They told me that my kids would say we had it all. Maybe they did, but I didn't.

I would leave because I did not feel right inside, and nobody ever says we get another chance at this thing called life. I was going to go after this second chance, and I would walk through fire to get there. When I got brave, I was tired of it all. Tired of being taken for granted and feeling like arm candy. The next time I had a real relationship, it would be a partnership; when we stood beside each other, we would be a motherfucking, powerhouse team. I would never walk behind someone or be invisible ever again.

The Transition

From being married to divorced, how can I describe it? As I sat at the dinner table with my children, eating without my ex was simply normal. It was normal because he had rarely eaten with us. I remember thinking that one night, thinking how I did not miss him because he was gone from my world in so many ways already. The biggest and hardest part was not seeing my kids. He was adamant that we were now "part-time parents." I hated that word. I wanted a transitional time for the kids to get used to not being with me, as I had been with them 100% of the time before the divorce. He didn't understand that.

I have one memory of him pulling my youngest out of my arms as she did not want to leave on one particular switch night. She cried so hard, and even today, it breaks my heart to think about it. I was so mad at myself for not using my voice that night to speak reason to him or at least try. I remember him saying, "You say kids are resilient, Jodi. She will be fine." I let him do that, and in this lifetime, I have very few regrets, but that is a huge one for me. I didn't fight for her; I was carrying so much guilt for breaking up our relationship that I let it happen.

This was the start of us doing a shit job of co-parenting. We were messing up the greatest parts of us, our children. Often when I heard negative words regarding myself, those were the words I held onto. Some of these words felt like footprints in wet concrete; I carried negative conversations about myself in my head for years, beating myself up that I was not a good enough mom anymore because I had selfishly picked me. This is where my internal dialogue would need so much work because I was carrying guilt for hurting all of them and thinking maybe I wasn't worth it. Maybe my job on Earth was supposed to be just taking care of them and keeping everything running smoothly, so it didn't matter. I didn't need to breathe or feel excitement because I was a piece of shit. I share with you this to show you that my internal demons were so real, and I had to change that dialogue or I would never grow, never truly experience what I believed in so passionately.

The woman you see today is not the woman I was ten, eight, six, or even five years ago. I had to put in the work, or I wouldn't have made it. I didn't even want to be here anymore at times. Thankfully, I had built grit in childhood, and I knew training was the one consistent thing I had control over. It saved me because I knew how to be strong, and I would fight every day to find peace within because at the end of the day, deep down inside, I loved Jodi. I knew I was kind, caring, funny, vivacious, full of light, and worthy!

Divorce: The Shit Storm

Roughly four years later, I had an evolving new company. It was a challenge on its own, and navigating a bad divorce was the extra life sauce I had to deal with. As funds were not abundant, when I had to go back to court, I decided to do the unthinkable and represent myself. Would I ever send you to get your car fixed without a mechanic? No, sure wouldn't, but I thought I could do it. Financially, I needed to do it.

Picture this: I was sitting in my SUV, listening to Rachel Platten's "Fight Song" while tears rolled down my face. Every word in that song represented so much to me. I had lost friends after the divorce. I was losing sleep and waking up feeling nauseous. My family was worried, and here I was sitting outside, ready to walk in alone to represent myself. I know what I was doing may not have been right, but I believed in the power of my voice, and maybe it was not about winning that day in court. Maybe it was about standing in my power and speaking my truth. I would not hide behind the fanciest lawyer in our city. I would stand my ground.

When I entered, his lawyer approached me about a deal. I kindly said, "No, thank you." Inside, I was screaming, *Fuck you!* This was the same lawyer who had gotten my ex to say I may have Munchausen syndrome by proxy, the disease where you want your children to be sick. My ex fully knew that I was the one who had found the research to get our daughter off TPN. I hated what divorce had done. The court appearance felt long and fast all at the same time. I didn't even know how to address the judge, and I quickly learned that I was slowly burying myself.

That day, I walked out of the courtroom in a daze. I kept walking down the street and looked up to find myself by the church. With snow on the ground, I went to the door to go in, but it was locked. I stood staring at the door handle, as I felt so defeated and broken. All I could think about was that even God was locking me out. I sat down and cried, and then I called my cousin Cory.

He answered right away. I said, "Cory, God has even locked me out!" I am not sure what he said other than, "Oh Jo, God hasn't locked you out." He likely said something fun or maybe,

"Oh fuck, that is quite the day you are having." I love this man. He is one of my favourite people on this Earth. My rock, my constant. We need these people when we feel we are at the bottom.

After I pulled myself together, I learned I did not need to enter a church to feel God in my life, and that with every lesson, I was to learn and take from it. I had and have a fire spirit inside me. Through my lessons of life, I am learning to not only navigate my life but also how to help others navigate theirs, as sharing our stories helps each other.

So today, if the "Fight Song" comes on when my daughters are driving around with their friends, they pretend to be me, lovingly mocking me and sending me Snapchats. Life of Jodi! Haha!

Round Two

Round two of being brought back to court came during the exciting time of the pandemic in 2020. This is how my pandemic year played out. The day I was looking at a potential studio space, I got a call from half a dozen clients saying that the "government was shutting us down." My first reaction was to let out a laugh of hysterics, like REALLY!! My second thought was, *Okay, how do I navigate this situation quickly?* I had by chance updated the online system in December because I had been working with a company out of the US with a potential to be on their app. Anyway, the system was there, ready. In forty-eight hours, I had all my studio clients and kettlebells, and by Friday at 5:30 p.m., we had our first online class! We Zoomed to talk momentarily before, then trained, then Zoomed again to see if everyone finished the workout. With my current clients taken care of, I now had to decide about the space.

My current rental space wanted rent for the months I would not be able to teach, and I have never been great at sitting still, so I agreed. We were able to negotiate a contract that gave us time. Hopefully, this would be short, and so the contracts were signed, and I would start renovations by June 2020. If the government let us open sooner, I would train clients outside until the space was ready. So, there was a lot going on.

I was not sure when we would be able to open. New space, new adventure? When we opened, could we stay open with Covid? Then came my surprise second court appearance. Would it ever STOP?

As this was all happening, my spousal support was ending. I was once told that I better find a man to take care of me, and that stuck in my brain and lived within my internal dialogue. I had always wanted to be independent and be able to take care of myself. I kept reminding myself that hurt people hurt people, but again, I tucked that piece of information in my mind and would have to work hard to let that go if I was to ever allow love in again.

I wanted to be independent, do it alone. This mentality to go it alone gave me great drive for my business, but it kept people who wanted to help, people who wanted to love me, at a distance. I was seeing someone at the time, and I never truly let him in because I held so much dislike for how men manipulate that I couldn't trust that he loved me. I pushed him away, and after that, I pretty much vowed to myself that I could walk this road alone and that my heart was better off numb versus shattered. I write this now with a different outlook and perspective, but it was where I was at the time.

The month when the spousal support stopped, I wondered if he would have a secret party with his girlfriend to celebrate being free from me. Okay, if the shoe was on the other foot, I totally would have celebrated starting a new chapter without the ex.

What happened next absolutely floored me. Not two days after that, I got a letter from his lawyer informing me that he was taking me to court. I was seriously thinking, *WHAT THE FUCK!* So much was going on ... The pandemic and now this. I couldn't figure out why.

Eleven months earlier, my family dynamic had changed when the kids had decided to move out. Out of respect for them, I won't go into this very much as I am confident their perspective is different, and it was such a hard time for all of us. This time, I felt yet again like a loser. I felt like they hated me and that they had chosen a side. I didn't understand how they could not stay with me.

My work was affecting EVERYTHING in my life on the grandest of scales! When my kids moved out, I threw myself into my passion, as it distracted me from the pain. I can actually describe the pain as losing the love of your life, your soulmate, your kindred spirit. I wanted to die. I was consumed with so many feelings and thoughts. I have never shared this, but at times, life was so dark when I was alone that I just thought, *Would anyone really miss me?* I had built this business, but a business is a business.

When this thought ever crossed my mind, I thought of one of my best friends who had lost loved ones to suicide. I could never do that to her, as I watched her struggle with the loss not once but two times. There were days I thanked God for her because she was my reality check. If she ever reads this, I want to thank her for being an important person in my life, for having given my head a shake to remind me that I had so much purpose and so much to offer the world, even if my kids had decided to move out.

Okay, now back to why I brought up that the kids didn't live with me. We were in the middle of a pandemic, I was working through if society would think I was a bad human being because my kids didn't pick me, and two days after spousal support ended, I got the letter from the lawyer for me to go back to court. My ex-husband wanted child support. I laughed, thinking, *Fuck, I can hardly buy groceries and I have a new company that might not even survive the pandemic, while he is a part owner of a real estate company.*

I tried to reach out to say that I wanted to help with the kids, but if he made me split my focus with having to go back to court, then I just wouldn't be able to do it. He refused to talk and only wanted to work through the lawyers. I decided that for round two, I would represent myself again, but this time, I would find a lawyer who would help me put together a case or at least give me an outline. 2020 was the craziest year of my life: pandemic, back to court, and the year of Rosie (I'll tell you about her later).

We were not allowed to go to court in person, so we would do it over the phone. With all my papers laid out on the counter, I had my mom with me and a really good friend. As my heart was pounding so loud, I thought again, *Oh shit, I can't even hear. Breathe, Jodi, breathe!* I don't remember much. I remember his lawyer doing something that quite upset the judge, and I thought, *Yes, this might work in my favour.*

Then I remembered I didn't have the best divorce lawyer in the city, and yet again, I was not a lawyer, but I was tapped out financially and emotionally. I wanted to say that day to the judge, "He has won … The kids live with him." If he wanted to hurt me, the pain was already so huge that whatever the outcome, it would only be about money, which I didn't have. In the end, it didn't turn out great, but it didn't turn out terrible either, kind of a 50/50 deal, so I was okay.

Honestly, at that point, I had been through so much, and I had still kept getting back up. I knew I could keep getting up because I was (and I am) strong. I learned so much about myself going through all of that. I learned that my release of frustration always took the form of tears in private, lying on the floor just crying. I remind myself I am no longer scared, as life seems to be like a wave. You ride or you crash; each are passing moments. I learned to embrace it and let it all out because I know I can get back up again, as my spirit is large and nothing can keep me down. I had so much healing to do, so much to finally sit down with to let go.

I learned that I wasn't managing my children properly as I had not set boundaries with them, and this was because I was carrying so much guilt that I had hurt them. I said to my mom one day, "If I do not let this go, it is going to destroy me completely." I would move forward, loving them always but no longer feeling guilty for wanting a life for myself. You raise your children to grow up and fly. You want them to fly, so you don't want to coddle them.

I finally realized I was an individual and had to see that because whether they were with me or not, one day, they would move on with their lives, so we were just fast-forwarding to that day. If there is any regret in my life, I say sorry and then move forward. I will no longer carry baggage like warrior metal. I want peace, and I choose peace because as a person, I deserve that too. In 2020, I opened my own studio space in the middle of a pandemic, I represented myself yet again in court, and I decided I was worthy of love again!

Scarecrow Festival

Thinking back on that day, it was a gift, the time spent with my youngest daughter at a scarecrow festival. The weather was as gentle as a soft embrace, and it felt like a day to connect with her. As we laughed and decided just to be together, not much could have made the day any better. As we strolled through the streets of the festival, she slipped her hand into mine. I didn't say anything as she was almost sixteen. It felt so similar to many times before, but it also felt different. It was like a reconnection to the love that had never escaped us, but at times had felt foreign and strange. I also had a moment when I reached across and touched the top of her head like I would have when she was little. I will never forget that day as it was such a gift. I didn't speak to her about how the memories were flooding back, as she was a teen, and I knew we were completely enjoying each other's company without the need for eye rolls or "Oh, Mom."

All these feelings would later leave me sobbing like a child in my vehicle soon after I dropped her off. I cried over lost time and the pain that I had wished I could remove from their memories. For over a year, I had apologized to them for not doing better at communicating with their dad and for my part in the divorce, as it takes two. It was my moment to let go and have peace with myself. Sitting there crying, I gently reminded myself to let go, but still, and even now, the sadness creeps in about not being around them all the time. I do not think that changes. I feel it just becomes less frequent. I was thinking about how my relationship with my children got scarred along the way, and yet how beautiful and peaceful the day was.

I work on healing my scars. They used to feel fresh and raw, and I would just wish at times they would build up enough scar tissue to get so hard that they would become numb. You know how it is to feel so much that you wish to be numb? I have felt that way so many times. Then I remind myself to live is to feel and to be numb is to be dead inside. Life is long and very sad if you wish for numbness.

CHAPTER 3:

REFLECTION

Connecting to the Mountains

My first solo road trip was to the mountains. I drove because I wanted to sing, laugh, and think. Windows rolled down as my AC was broken. I headed out for my seven-hour drive. My first stop was Medicine Hat. I went to a provincial park, and my task was to read. Now, it sounds funny, but ever since my separation, I hadn't been able to read. I could not sit still and quiet my mind enough to read.

Then I found this book, *The Untethered Soul* by Michael Singer. (I use it in my Kettlebell Kickboxing challenges even today.) The book is never far from me to this day. I can always open it up and read, and it helps me. Anyway, I read that day. I was working on being still and slowing my mind so that I could connect with myself again. So, I lay in the sun and read. I was so excited as I love to read and felt relieved to gain this back.

I think when we are in turmoil, we often busy ourselves so much that we can't really fix our problems because we are never slow enough to even recognize they exist. I highlighted this sentence in the book, and I believe it is true regarding why we have to slow down, stop avoiding our pain, and acknowledge it instead: "If you are doing something to avoid pain, then pain is running your life. All of your thoughts and feelings will be affected by your fears" (Singer 2013, 100).

My next stop was the Rockies! I had a cup of coffee, of course, as it was now my tradition to drive into the mountains with a coffee and great music! I would go for a hike, and sit, and think. If you have ever been to the mountains or the ocean, you will understand the energy that flows there. A place to connect to the earth, to the universe, to yourself. A moment always hits me, even today, when I am there. I look way up and realize how tiny I am in the big universe. It is humbling to realize you are of little importance in the grand scheme of things. Nature makes you very aware of how quickly things change. It is a place to find oneness within me. On that day, it allowed me to breathe, to think, and to start learning how to be quiet in my mind and my body.

Often, when I now leave or enter the mountains, I will cry. Not because I am sad but because my first trip here brought me so much peace within, and the mountains will forever call me back as if they are part of my home within.

Dealing with High Anxiety

I can tell you that as a child, I had severe anxiety, and I never really told anyone. It would hit me like a brick; I would feel like all the walls were closing in, and I couldn't breathe. Back then, people didn't talk much about mental wellness. I figured out on my own that movement and fresh air were my friends.

I remember often leaving the house quietly to go outside just to find space to breathe.

When I divorced, I struggled to eat in smaller restaurants or to be in them for too long, but I was agitated and needed to eat and get out. I recall being in a restaurant in Calgary with my best friend, Krissy. She would look at me with kindness, not saying anything, but I always felt like we didn't have to speak. When she looked at me with such kindness, she was holding space for me, and without words, her look was always reassuring and communicating, "I'm right here, and you are doing great." After going through all I have gone through, I am reminded that people don't need solutions or words—we just want that hand to hold or that person to sit with us and remind us that we are not alone.

Long after when many of the stories you will read here occurred, anxiety sometimes came back tenfold for me. Running a business as a female, I would go to bed and wake up feeling quite similar to when I went through divorce—feeling like I wanted to vomit. It would escalate, and then I would nervous cough and make myself gag. Then I would remember my dad doing the same thing when I was a small child, and here I was, dealing in the same way. Training made it feel better during the day, but every night and every morning, I would lay in bed worrying about money and how I was going to do it all.

Then one day, I decided I needed something to hold on to, and I did not want it to be another person as I wished to be whole first before I let someone in. So I decided to pray. I would go to bed, and my anxiety would creep in, and I would repeat the Lord's Prayer over and over and over, until my nerves settled or I fell asleep. I am not overly religious, but I do believe in a higher power, and God seems to fit with me.

I am a very physical person, and I miss physical touch from a partner, but again, after years of feeling alone while laying beside someone, I know that filling a space with someone just to have someone is not going to fix that feeling. To be complete, you need to fill that space on your own.

On the really hard nights, I will pray, and I will imagine God's arms around me, or I will ask the universe to place me in its arms so that I can feel as one and sleep. This might sound crazy, but many people ask me how I do it, and this is how I do it. I need to be whole for myself, and as my business and my life ebbs and flows, my anxiety is at different levels. I am learning as I go.

I have also learned a very big lesson: In an instant, life can be halted, and so I let the fear of failure fall away a bit more. Money plays a big role in our lives as we need it to survive and to be free. As I strive for freedom, and financial freedom specifically, I use gratitude to recognize that the most precious and most valuable things are not the dollar signs. I know as long as I am healthy and able to work, I am rich beyond many. With that richness, I write to share my exercises, I teach, and I connect, so I can be of service and hold space for others just as people have done for me. I have had lots of trial and error in learning how to deal with my anxiety and panic attacks, which happen on a smaller scale and more rarely today because I work at being level. Less highs mean less lows! I celebrate small victories, but I celebrate the journey even more!

The Health Scare

In April 2019, my doctor informed me that my Pap test came back abnormal. I thought, *Well, here we go.* I know what stress does to the body; our bodies can only carry us through so long before it suffers. I was in the middle of a nasty divorce, I had just moved my kids out of their childhood home, and I was starting a new business while trying to maintain my stay-at-home-mom status with my children—I was exhausted to say the least. I was told I had to wait six months to see if it would grow into something more—*Like frick, now I have to wait.* I don't like waiting for anything. I understood you could have abnormal cells if you were run-down. I thought, *Ok, I get it, but how am I going to navigate this one?* Things with my kids weren't great: First, I had left their dad, and now I had moved them out of the only home they knew, plus I was seeing someone.

I didn't tell them anything as I didn't want them to think I was playing the victim, so I decided to keep the findings to myself and wait and see what the doctor said next. I told my mom and a few of my friends, but other than that, I just kept moving forward. Life went on, and it would be the year that my kids decided to go live with their dad full-time.

I then found out that I needed a procedure to investigate further the abnormal cells. I knew one thing: I am a fighter, and I would fight hard if I needed to. I also needed to find ways to destress. I moved that summer to a new apartment in Regina, a place I fell in love with and called my home. As the landlord let me, I was greeted by a puppy. I thought, *Oh my God, I can get a dog!* The unique thing about looking for a place was I was also looking for me. I opened the door, and the light beamed in ... I fell in love! I said, "No need to show me any more. It's perfect for me and my new future!"

So, I had a new home, a place for me to focus on Jodi, a place to watch the sunrise, and a place to love my body, so if I had to fight, I would! As time evolved, I ended up having what they call a Loop Electrosurgical Excision Procedure (LEEP). They describe it as using something like a melon ball scooper to hopefully scoop out all the bad parts. Notice here the word "hopefully"—you've got to have hope and faith because you only ever have two options: faith or fear. I choose faith time and time again. Your body needs faith, love, and healing!

In February of 2020, as I was getting ready for the procedure, I had still not shared with my kids that they had found abnormal cells. I thought, *Why worry them at this point?* I didn't want them to feel sorry for me because that made me feel gross. I always find myself pulling away from people to persevere, especially when I am worried. Although, I know I am strong and healthy! My mom dropped me off. I got to the room, and I was feeling very odd as one does laying on a bed naked except for a robe, with people ready to look at your privates in a medical way. (Having children teaches you how to prepare yourself for these moments when your body is simply a body, nothing more and nothing less.)

My doctor was phenomenal. I asked her what she needed from me. I also was in a twenty-one-day virtual challenge with an ex-Navy SEAL, Thom Shea, whom I had met on LinkedIN. This was my first challenge I was to do with Thom. I was also doing the challenge with two of my kettlebell trainers. I was supposed to finish the day with push-ups, sit-ups, and squats. I also needed to be back on the mats teaching. My doctor looked at me without ever pushing me, but she simply said, "I need you to give your body twenty-four hours of rest." I agreed, knowing I would fail the challenge and have to restart and own it the following week. However, I was good with it because

I trusted my doctor, and she wasn't asking me to pause for a crazy long time.

She then said, "Now, I'm going to paint this solution onto your cervix. It's going to feel cool, and then you are going to be hit with an adrenaline rush." She was not kidding. I first felt the cool, then I felt like it ran from my stomach to my heart. All of a sudden, my heart was racing, and I felt like my ears were pounding. All I could think about was my kids and that I was so scared in that moment. I was thinking, *Oh my God, I didn't tell them I was having this LEEP. What if my heart just explodes?*

Of course, it didn't, but in those quick seconds, I made some really big decisions on how to move forward. I realized it is not playing a victim to tell people you love that you are having a procedure. It's important to have people love and support you. I realized all of this laying on that bed.

I also had to go into a meeting and tell the ex-Navy SEAL and my two trainers that I hadn't done the exercises that night because I had felt terrible. He asked me if my back was broken, and then he said that just because a doctor told me to rest that didn't mean I had to listen, and that I could have broken up the exercises and completed them. I am aware of my commitment to my life, to my training, and to my internal dialogue, but I asked what the doctor needed for me to take care of ME, and I choose that day to rest. Failing the challenge set by a SEAL was not easy, but in a way, it was easy because I had made the decision to take twenty-four hours and then own that decision. I would start at day one again, and I knew I would finish it because I am true to my word. And I did!

Twenty-Four-Hour Walking Challenge with an Ex-Navy SEAL

After working and training virtually with an ex-Navy SEAL, Thom Shea, I decided to take him up on his invite to travel to Greenville, South Carolina in October 2021 for his twenty-four-hour walking challenge. My goals on that trip and challenge were to find a way to level up my business, break through the barriers, and conquer.

Fifteen hours into the challenge, I was encouraged to connect with another SEAL to get guidance on how to level up. I was so excited to connect and see what I was about to learn. My time had arrived! Roughly three walking paces into meeting this man, he blurted out, "Tell me about your divorce!" I paused, thinking, *Did I just hear him right? I must be tired.* I replied, "Really? Well, it's kind of like beating a dead horse. Is it necessary?" (Now, the terminology of "beating a dead horse" must be Southern slang because written it looks off . . . I digress again.) He explained that until I dealt with it, I wouldn't be able to level up. He proceeded to tell me that I have zero immediate family support for what I am trying to build. I understood that part, and so my heart fell a bit as I walked, talked, and listened. He said that I needed to go home and ask for forgiveness. I needed to say I was sorry for my part.

Later on, we would all sit and listen to Thom again, so I left my walking partner, thinking about how I'd go back to him again . . . and speak my thoughts. Insert growth: I grew up not liking confrontation, so I would go quiet. Now, I wasn't quiet. I walked for a bit, then I met up with him again, and I told him, "I think you are wrong. I don't need to go down that road again." He said he disagreed.

I finished the challenge, and the next day, I was angry because I had come for business and instead I was thinking about my past—the shit I had left behind. Then, as the day dragged on, I asked myself a very pivotal question: *Jodi, why are you angry? If you had dealt with this, then it should not bother you anymore. You should be able to let it go and walk forward.* After I asked myself the question, I knew the answer. I needed to go back and speak with my ex and my children. I needed to say sorry for my part and ask for forgiveness. I thought, *Oh my God, I'm back here again!* So when I landed, I laid out my next four days in my head. I would speak to each of them so I could let go, move on, make peace within myself, and unchain myself from the anchor. I knew the process, and I knew the importance of it. So, I had four days, and I am a doer. I got it done!

The conversations were real. I remember when I told my son we needed to talk, he said, "Do we have to?" My answer was this: "I know talking is hard at times, but I would rather do hard now then let it sit. When you don't speak about how you feel, when you let words go unspoken, things fester, they don't go away. And if you can speak about them, they often lose their power and you can let it go freely." I think the conversation with one of my girls took place while sitting on a curb, and the conversation with my ex? Well, that was through a text. I sent that text for myself to make peace, not for a reply or a reaction. I had learned that when we make peace, it has to be within; you do not get peace from others.

A Letter to the Other Woman

In March of 2023, when my children left with their dad to attend his wedding, I wrote this letter to the other woman, the woman who would become my children's stepmom.

Dear New Stepmom,

Years ago, I was told that you were to be the positive and strong role model for my children that I was not. I hated you that day, without even knowing you. I was asked quite quickly if I would like to meet you, and if I wanted to introduce my new partner too. There was no new partner in my life, but I didn't want to meet you. I did creep you. I did open my ears wide when the children brought up your name. I know I didn't hate you, yet you reminded me of what I was not. I was not the woman with the Monday to Friday career who would fit so much better into my children's lives. I wondered if that made me a bad mom, a bad woman. I would carry this in my internal dialogue, and when I had bad days, I would use myself as a punching bag and beat myself up. I thought you were what my kids needed, and I was not.

I was unfamiliar to them as I was trying to grow my business. You were fitting the mold that I could not. I had to find peace in my mind and within myself. I was reminded that when we were kids, we had multiple moms and dads, these were our best friends' parents. We would call them our other parents as they loved us and took care of us like their own. I reminded myself that if you love my children, it would only benefit them as it takes a village to raise children. I did not hate you, but I hated myself. As I got stronger and as I felt more love for myself, you no longer became a threat, just another person to hopefully strengthen and enrich their lives. I still feel jealous when I know you get to spend time with them when I cannot, but that is a me thing to work on.

I will likely never have coffee with you as a friend, but in my mind, I do not hold anger or fear that you are the other woman in their lives. I ask that you cherish your time with them as it is the most precious gift on this planet. Love them as if they were your own, but I ask you to be respectful that they do have a mom, someone who put Band-Aids on scratches, hooked up TPN machines, taught them how to throw a pitch and ride a two-wheeler, and who is still present and here. We may not interact, but we will be better without hate and with mutual respect. As you become their stepmom, I hope you hold the label with the utmost privilege, and I wish you a lifetime of memories with them.

From the Original Mom

Owning Me

We talk about speaking our vulnerabilities, yet often it is something we are uncomfortable with sharing. I often thought being vulnerable was a weakness that I did not want, and I definitely did not want to share, until I realized the strength within vulnerability. I believe now that strength cannot exist without vulnerability, and that is a beautiful thing, even though it is uncomfortable for me. I was not going to write about this in-depth because it was something I experienced that was so painful and so embarrassing. Then I reminded myself that the reason I am sharing is to be real and vulnerable. This past year, I shared this experience with another divorced mom. Afterward, she said, "I understand because that happened to me too." Often we hold shit inside, embarrassed and hurt, but I think the true power of sharing is that it allows us to see we are not alone so we can let go of some of the pain we carry.

So, I will share my saddest time in the last ten years, when my children decided to move out full-time. My world was rocked, and I decided it was time to numb my heart. I call it my biggest heartbreak because my children are my greatest love. I think I am not alone in this feeling; when you have children, your love for them is so large that you get lost in them and forget to remain separate. After they left, there were moments when I couldn't breathe, and my work was all I had.

I was so embarrassed, as I always felt the greatest bond is that of a mother and her children. I felt like I must have been the worst mom in the world, and that they couldn't stand to be with me. I felt like a failure and a terrible mom. I remember being so good at it, so it broke my heart to think I wasn't anymore. I was so fearful of the time I was going to lose, time that I knew I would never get back. I would have to find a way to trust the love and faith I had instilled in my children, and then pray we would find our way back to one another.

I often talked to my mom about my worries on how society would view me. We all say we want to go through this life not caring what people think. You get older, and they say you care less. I don't think this is true. I think we should care about the opinions of those who matter to us. The people near and dear to me understood because they knew the situation, and they knew me. As for the people who didn't understand, their thoughts and opinions didn't matter to me. I don't think this is an age thing that teaches you to let go; when you spend time working on yourself, you slowly figure things out.

When I decided to let go of what I thought things should look like, I stopped trying to parent my children in the smaller moments because the moments were few. I decided if I got three hours a week in their space, I would just love them in those moments. Our family looked different. When I stopped pushing and stopped trying so hard, it allowed me to heal and connect better. All families look different, and mine would be uniquely its own.

I also realized that a heart is supposed to love, and even though at times, mine hurt so bad I wished to numb it completely, I knew then I wouldn't be living life. It's like the lyric in "Iris" by the Goo Goo Dolls: "You bleed just to know you're alive."

Thoughts on a Plane

Coming back from a trip to Toronto, I was thinking of my beautiful children, as I often do, and the words began to roll.

To My Children,

I close my eyes, inhale, and catch a jagged breath as I exhale. So many lessons life has taught me. As a child, it taught me love but also fear—to be silent inside and to not trust. I carried much of this into my young adulthood without even knowing. When I became your mom, it was the greatest gift I had ever been given because I was going to be the best at it, and I was, then I wasn't. Your youth is burned into my mind.

Connor, the lisp you had that frustrated you, and your big blue eyes that were also so excited and full of wonder. Your independence scared me as I wanted to keep you little forever. I did so much wrong with you, and you were the one I wanted to always do so much right for.

Mira, God gifted you, and my job became to be your protector, your doctor, and your nurse . . . I was ready to be your everything. I was wrong, as I was supposed to be your angel to guide you, watch you, and walk along holding your hand when you needed it. I wasn't supposed to teach you to worry or be super careful. I look at you and still see that little, sweet girl with stains on her teeth who was so damn cute. I am so freaking grateful you didn't have to be hooked up to a machine, and that you simply existed on the Earth when, at times, I thought God would take you.

Ava, you are my added blessing ... the little girl whose hand fit so perfectly into mine. The one who always had a smile and a temper to match if the world did not get what you were meaning. I can close my eyes and see the years I got to stay home with you, and I see those years as one of my greatest gifts. I know the changes that pushed me to build something confused you and made you feel secondary, but this was so far from the truth. I just wanted to do better for you and for me.

When I left, my soul was crushed because I could not support you. I felt I had failed you. I watched a spark go out of you when we told you our family was separating and I feared I would never find my way back to you. As life guided me, I threw myself into my work to save my heart from breaking. KBKB saved me from dying of a broken heart because my babies were no longer with me. I did not realize the depth of this until later. I would spend time with you, and then when you would leave, I would do only what kept me from falling to pieces on the floor—work.

I cannot change the past, but I can learn from it. As my children, you know the impact it has had on me, and God knows the impact it has had on your lives. Again, when we share, my hope is to remind us that we are not alone in it. We learn by making mistakes, and we provide comfort by sharing. I write this as I fly home from a weekend in Toronto. I am happy to be wearing a mask as tears are streaming down my face as well as other disgusting fluids from my nose! Haha, sorry, TMI.

If I was to share knowledge with you, it would be this:

I wish you to know that life is made up of mistakes, so find empathy because we never really know about life or why it happens the way it does, not until we have a similar experience, then we are blessed with an aha moment. Experience teaches us so much.

I was glad I could stay at home with you as little children, and I am grateful every day to your dad for that gift. I am sorry some of life's unfortunate lessons came from your parents who did not know better.

I wish for you to find love, the greatest of loves, and to find something you are passionate about so that you can dream big and pursue those dreams like it was the only thing keeping you breathing. I wish you moments of solitude, as I believe we learn so much about ourselves and life in quiet.

Be instead of do ... Become aware of what is around you. Life is short, and life is long—both are hard. Be grateful for all little things that unknowingly turn out to be the big things. I know each of you have been blessed with a uniqueness to bring to the world ... Listen, it is inside you, and only you can unlock it. Once unlocked, then you must figure out how to share and use it.

I love you to the moon and back. Though my job is not to fix, I will always hold space for you and hold your hand when you need it.

Love,

Mom

CHAPTER 4:

UNBECOMING

Stress and Weight Loss

What do I mean by *unbecoming*? Throughout life, we have transitions, and we take on these roles, such as wife, mom, and coworker. I recently chatted with my niece, and she said, "Auntie, I think about who you were back then, and I see you now, and I see such a different person." Many of us think that as we grow and work on ourselves, we change into someone new, and we do to a point. I believe when we work on ourselves, we uncover the real, authentic self. We dispose of these layers (who we thought we needed to be), layers that were covering the authentic self. Instead of embracing our true self, we take on the roles: mother, wife, sister, friend, coworker . . . instead of funny, caring, charismatic, determined, playful, loyal, fierce, and loving.

Everyone deals with stress differently. Some of us overeat, and some of us undereat. We simply develop bad habits because we do not know how to deal with stress. On top of this, the automatic stress response of fight, flight, or freeze kicks in. To be fair, I think if you were not taught strategies as a child,

I mean *healthy* strategies, then how are you to know what to do until you get dragged through the mud a few times and finally figure it out?

When I was so stressed, I had no motivation to eat. I would simply eat just to make my body function. I had zero desire to eat. I remember the day I took my kids on a trip, and we were going zip-lining. You had to weigh over 100 lb. or else you would need someone to zip with you. I got on the scale and weighed in at 103 lb. That number scared me. I had not been that light since Mira had been sick. I remember the moment vividly: As I looked up from the scale, I caught my son looking up at me after checking the scale himself with those beautiful blue eyes. I was struggling, and he likely knew it.

Kids are smart. We think they don't know things, but they do. I was ashamed of my weight loss. I was struggling and felt ashamed in knowing that I was likely not hiding it well from the ones I loved most in the world. I grew up thinking that if I pushed my trauma away and didn't share it with the world, then that trauma would exist less. I thought nobody knew, but then I suffered in silence. I knew deep down they saw me struggling to find my way.

One night, the kids were at their dad's, and I was making dinner for myself. I called my dear friend Krissy in Calgary, and I burst into tears, saying, "I don't know how to cook for one person." Now realistically, I am an educated, intelligent woman, so I know how to cook for one or twenty people, but life had me derailed, and triggers were happening everywhere. I did not want to eat, and when I went to eat on my week off from the kids, I would be sobbing because I mentally felt I couldn't cook for one. My triggers were in the driver's seat of my life, and I needed to find a way to take back the wheel.

The beauty of writing this book is not to hide behind a big smile or a strong, sculpted body but to share the story that built the woman as some refer to as "the lady who swings the kettlebell." So, eating was hard, and I had a world of work and healing to do. Like training, my focus was not always one push-up at a time but one healthy, full meal at a time. I used techniques and methods to unwind myself from triggers in order to take back my life.

I would love to sit here and tell you it was quick and easy, but it wasn't. It was so hard. At times, I felt so much pain that I would feel numb. The one thing that I can tell you is that it is so worth it, all the work to get to a better place, to see the beauty in each day and find yourself again. Sometimes, we just don't know how to find ourselves, and sometimes, there is so much darkness that we cannot see the light. I think it's wise to start with small, healthy habits, and then allow those habits to grow little by little. This might be as simple as getting outside once a day to breathe, as nature will help you heal. Think of your journey as a journey of unbecoming.

Five Years to Normal?

Not a lot of people in my circle of friends were divorced: my brother and my cousin, but as for close friends, none. Back when I was newly divorced, a friend connected me with a lady who had divorced about five years prior. She met me for lunch one day. I call her my angel. She sat and listened and gave me advice on how to navigate it, reminding me that what I was going through was normal and I wasn't crazy. She then said that in about five years, it would settle down. I was like, *What the fuck? If I have to deal with this for that long, I am never going to make it!* She reassured me it was a "process." I left thinking, *A process . . . A baby is born and is running and going to school in the fifth year of life . . . What will my life be like?* There were moments of pain at a turtle-like pace, but I want to fast-forward for a moment, approximately yes, five years.

After launching my business, I became very active on social media. I had started following a martial arts company called Budo Brothers, and I would comment on their content once in a while. Eventually, one of the owners reached out to me. His name was Kyle. He wanted to add to his portfolio as he also had a marketing company. He reached out suggesting that the next time I was in Calgary, he could shoot free content for me if he could also use it. He recommended doing some urban photos followed by a day shoot in the Canadian Rockies. Now it is not as if I knew nothing about him, so I wrote back, *Great, let's do it.*

Until that point, I had done one little photo shoot in Regina, and I had done a bigger one in NYC, but I had never organized my own, so I was excited, and it was FREE! I say I gently dip my toes into all my projects, but I always ask myself, *Will I regret saying no?* It was a great opportunity because as a new business owner, I knew content creation with photography and videography is super expensive.

When I arrived Thursday night, he called and asked if I would like to accompany him to his ninjutsu class, and I said that of course I would. My kids always freak out, saying I am very trusting, but I have learned not to be foolish, to be wise but to trust my gut. My friends always knew where I was.

Turns out, the class was incredible. I was beginning to become very familiar with doing things outside my comfort zone. Equally incredible that night was Kyle being tested for his black belt. It was one of the coolest things I have ever gotten to watch. Afterward, I looked at him and said, "Had I known you were such a ninja, I might have thought twice about agreeing to go into the mountains alone with you!"

Kyle picked a tunnel for the midday shoot. I was walking through, and I turned and looked over my shoulder to see the light at the end. My heart surely skipped a beat. I had found my purpose and my passion, and there was the light at the end of the tunnel, literally and figuratively. It had taken me time to get to this moment, but I had gotten there.

How did I get to the light at the end of the tunnel? I decided to just be me—discover who Jodi was and who she wasn't. I was tired of spinning my wheels and listening to everyone's opinion on who I needed to be. So I decided I wasn't going to decide on anything. I would find an appreciation for smelling flowers (literally), watching sunrises and sunsets, and being grateful for having breath inside me.

I smiled looking at the light at the end of the tunnel and holding the kettlebell in my hand. I could feel the weight as I stood there, and I remembered how I had felt when I'd picked up the kettlebell for the first time. It had felt oddly familiar in my hands. In all my chaos, the world had gone quiet. I had been completely in the zone and happy. I can't explain it other than saying I had known this part of my journey had been waiting for me to find it.

We then spent the rest of the day in the mountains shooting. He kept asking to carry my kettlebell, and I kept refusing. I had not realized the walls of independence I had built, especially around men. I finally gave him the kettlebell, as I recognized his kindness was not to be interpreted as a threat. I had a lot of walls I was learning to dismantle. As we walked down the mountain, he looked over at me and said, "Thank God you didn't take advantage of me and throw me in the forest!" I laughed so hard.

This adventure taught me so much. I was put in that tunnel to reflect on my journey. Most importantly, it taught me to let my walls down and to allow people to help me. I did not know it at the time, but I had found a best friend for life. Living only a province away, Kyle has since done more photos for me, and he has sat with me on many calls, either to strategize or to ask if I was okay. I have not let many men into my life, but I am grateful for him every day, and I wish him the most glorious, successful, and happy life!

The Whisper

I think there is a whisper within us all, but we often get too busy and simply stop listening to it. I used to keep myself so busy to avoid pain that I never paused. My uncle once said to me, "Practice sitting quietly, as this is when you will heal and find peace." During this time, I would move constantly because I couldn't stand the quiet. Remember, I went from a house of five every day to me alone every other week. The silence made me stir-crazy. It was as if I was afraid to be in my own skin. I think of it now, and my heart rate actually increases. I have to take a deep breath and remind myself I am not there; I am here and present.

The whisper will never come in the busy chaos, or at least it didn't for me. It came as I began getting comfortable in my own skin again. It is so incredible to write this, as I can spend so much time alone now and crave it when it used to scare me.

The whisper for me was the connection with the kettlebell. The day I picked up that kettlebell and felt its weight, I felt grounded, like it had a large purpose for me. I didn't know the specifics, but there was a path for me. I listened then, and I still listen today. It whispers for me to keep knowing that my purpose is strongly rooted within, and it will continue to unfold as I move forward. I think we all have this, and I think we all search for it. I found my whisper when I stopped seeking my purpose and just decided to be Jodi and let life unfold. When stress and worry is high, I sit quietly, close my eyes, and feel the guidance and the whisper.

The Phoenix

I had contemplated for years about getting a phoenix tattoo, and in 2022, I finally got one. As you know, it symbolizes the rise from the ashes. It is how I have felt about my life, or at least how I was waiting to feel about it. I kept putting it off because I never felt like I had risen "enough," until I sat with a thought. I had published several articles in magazines, I had opened a studio in the middle of a pandemic, I had created a hybrid model that put my company on the global platform, and I'd flown to train with an ex-US military ... Why did I not think I had risen enough? Was I not happy with the success I had?

I kept thinking and thinking, and then I came to this realization: What if this was it? What if I had risen? Why must I always think it needed to be harder for me to attach the symbol that I had done well. So I booked the appointment. I decided through that process that part of the journey, part of the success, is the present moment. What if this is how it looks? I know I will strive for new levels, but I was learning that I must value my here and now to embrace happiness and peace.

The tattoo was going to be on my left side, reaching my left armpit and including parts of my left breast. When I arrived, I realized, *Oh my God, what should I have worn?* Like a bikini top would have been great, but that's hindsight again! The tattoo artist said, "No worries, go into the bathroom. Here are two sheets of white hospital paper." (You know the kind they give you when going for a Pap test? Okay, men, the kind when you go for your physical.) Anyway, this was like two small squares. He handed me tape and said, "Use this to cover your breasts." I giggled in the bathroom in my attempt to create a proper cover. You know, tape doesn't stick very well to skin, but it would have to do. I came out and thought, *Wow, fashion statement, Barrett!*

Once we got started, I couldn't have cared less if my breast had fallen out as I had my legs up in a fetal position, and I was swearing like a trucker, so my breasts falling out became less of a concern. A guy walked in and sat down. He asked if I wanted him to hold my hand. I think I rolled my eyes. Honestly, I was worried I would crush his hand, and I was focusing on breathing and not being tense. Anyway, I survived the humbling experience of laying on a tattoo table while completely exposed, but I love my tattoo!!

Modeling

In the winter of 2023, I got a text from my friend Kyle. He randomly wrote, *Jodi, why don't you reach out to a modeling agency? You are posting images anyways, and you love clothes, so why don't you at least get paid for what you are already doing??* When I was a little girl, I did not necessarily have dreams of getting married, but I had thought about modeling, but it had never been more than a thought. So that day, I threw it back to him and wrote, *Sure, but who?* I was thinking he wouldn't have an answer for me, but then he immediately sent me a link.

I often do things immediately on the spot as my days get busy, and I don't want to forget. So I opened the link and realized I needed to send them one image. I asked him, *Can you help me pick it?* We decided on a bikini photo with my outrageous looking furry jacket! Then I went about my day attending a friend's birthday. As the meal ended, I glanced down at my phone as an email came in. I skimmed it quickly, and it was the agency requesting an interview the following Tuesday!

I closed the email and smiled to myself. When I got home later, I sent Kyle a text: *I got a freaking interview!* I sat there that night going back through all I had learned. You will always get a no if you don't even try. I spoke to my daughter about the power of putting it out there. I had written things and thought that was where the power came from, but I finally understood that if I am thinking it in my mind, it is out there. Be careful what you write *and* what you think because the power is incredible. I never wrote I wanted to model, but I thought about it, especially as I thought about magazine covers for my business, and then now, here I am.

The Photo Shoot

Whenever doubt creeps in, like it did on my first portfolio shoot, I say, "Why not me? Why can't I have huge success?" I say this out loud instead of beating myself up and feeling defeated.

The afternoon I went to the photo shoot, I was very professional, or at least to the extent that I can be—seriously, I am ridiculous because it is my nature! I packed so many clothes, which they had said must be on individual hangers. I flew to Calgary with no garment bags. Now, imagine me with probably fifteen outfits, maybe more. I was wearing a hat because they had said to bring props!

I walked onto the street in my long, black, seamless, fitted dress and total commando underneath because they had specified, "No tight clothes and no lines!" I laughed because there is a first time for everything, and I would have no lines. Internally, I was thinking, *Okay, I hope they don't just want me to change on the spot because I am going to be totally naked.* Anyway, that was some of my internal dialogue and how I was "following guidelines"! I was looking for my Uber and feeling free—like literally!

I saw a Corolla pull up. I walked confidently over and opened the back door. The guy looked at me and said, "I am not Uber!" I laughed at myself and said, "Oh, shit!" But I was thinking, *Okay, but my Uber is late, so maybe you can give me a ride?* I kept that to myself as I felt I may have infringed on his boundaries already! My Uber arrived and took me to my shoot.

The photo shoot was running behind, and so they told me to leave my stuff and go across the street for a coffee. I love coffee, so off I went. As I was getting coffee, I thought about how I loved getting old, as it had given me confidence; my nerves had settled, and I was just ready to embrace the experience. I texted my colleague and new coach: *I love that age has given me this feeling of confidence.* He wrote back, *Is it really age?* I smiled and quickly replied, *No, it has nothing to do with age. I am so happy I have worked so hard on myself, and that I love myself, and I am super proud of myself.* Yes, these are the thoughts and conversations that happen in my day! I think he sent me check marks and a bull's-eye emoji.

Back at the shoot, I got my makeup done. While she did that, I convinced her kettlebell training was the way to go. We exchanged Insta! She did my makeup quite naturally, but it still felt like a mask. I reminded myself that they were the professionals, and I got to play that day. I briefly met one of the owners, who immediately introduced herself and told me that she loved my eyes. I quickly thought about how I have my dad's eyes. I had never thought much of my eyes at all, but I used to think, as a kid, *I wish I had my dad's eyes.* Turns out, I do.

The shoot was pretty basic, but then the photographer said, "Want to put on something fun?!" I was all over that. I do have a bit of zest for life and FUN. Oh yes, I had the perfect outfit for that. Black tutu, strapless top, and pink high-top runners!! That screamed fun!

The photographer was great. He had great cues on how to move my head and body. As a trainer, I thought to myself, *Hmmm ... How can I use that cue?* He told me that I reminded him of Jennifer Aniston. I giggled, thinking, *Did they pay him to say that?* But I didn't care because it made me feel good. I thanked him. He then told me that it was best for me to be smiling in photos because my smile was incredible.

Now, I am not sharing this to feel shiny and bright, yet I do. I think we often dull our shine to fit in, but I have decided that I don't want to fit in. I want to be uniquely Jodi, and I want you to be uniquely you because that is what makes you special.

Now, back to the smile, as I have a story I want to share with you. When I was about nineteen, my dad wrote me an apology letter. He told me how proud he was of me and how much he loved me. It came after a very hard, life-changing moment. I keep the letter beside my bed in my nightstand, not because I read it all the time, but because it reminds me to heal, let go, and make the choice to be free.

In the letter, which brings me back to the smile, my dad wrote that God had gifted me the most beautiful smile that was to be shared with the world, and that he did not want to see any more tears. Whenever someone comments on my smile or my eyes, I think of my dad. I think of how we had to grow, heal, and move forward. He taught me so much. He was and is tough and resilient, and I love him very much.

So when the photographer said my best look was my smile, I smiled and thanked him, knowing that I was gifted it to share. If my smile can help light someone else's day, then I will smile often and always. My purpose has been to help others find their smile inside and out!

Where will the photo shoot take me? It will take me wherever I focus on. I have an idea, and I think writing this at forty-seven shows that there is no stopping me! Why not me?!

CHAPTER 5:

INTEGRITY

The Bungee Jump

Back in the summer of 2014, I was dating someone, and we decided to bungee jump. I had never done it, but I think when you go through pain and heartache, you fear dying less because you've already hurt so much.

I truly got over my fear of flying at the point in my life when I thought I was crawling through the mud. I was in turbulence and thinking, *Well, my life is kind of shitty right now, so I don't even care.* It was a scary place to be. At the same time, it was the place I grew from, the place where I let fear fall away and not have such a big hold on my life. I would never not complete or try something because of fear. I would recognize fear. I would not ignore the signs, but I would process it differently.

When I decide I am going to do something, I do it, and that is that. When I went to the top to bungee jump that day, I noticed the guy had given the girl before me a little push. I was infuriated. When it came to my turn, I looked at him and said,

"If you take away my ability to do this on my own by pushing me, I will walk back up these stairs after and punch you."

He stood back. With my heartbeat in my throat, I jumped. I screamed loudly for the entire time until I was safely and slowly dangling upside down. I had forgotten something at the top and had to walk back up those stairs. When I got to the top, he said, "Longest scream I have ever heard." I smiled and thanked him.

You see, I no longer want anyone to be responsible for my successes and my failures. I carry these on my shoulders. For every bad relationship I have been in, it was my choice. If I let shitty in, then I have to own that. We spend a lifetime tossing the buck and making excuses. When I got stronger, I told myself there were no more excuses; it was time to start owning where I was currently standing, so I could make changes to better myself.

Six-Day Job

In 2014, when I was newly divorced, the struggle to find myself a job and make money created a lot of stress. After eleven years of being a stay-at-home mom, I suddenly needed what society viewed as a "real job"! Don't get me started, as the best gig and most important one is to raise our children, yet it's not considered to be a job. Regardless of my thoughts, I needed a job. With the struggle to find myself and make money, I was stressed but found my first job rather quickly.

I applied and was hired at a dental office. It was close to home, plus it had benefits and was stable in the eyes of society. Six days in, I called my cousin and said, "I fucking hate it, but I can't quit?" I couldn't stand the office drama. I couldn't believe how much drama could live in such a small business. Sitting was something I was not fond of, "trying to look busy" was exhausting, and going through files of teeth (like real teeth) made me want to literally gag.

I don't quit easily, contrary to my family believing that I woke up one day and said, "Today is a great day to leave my marriage." I have been raised to give it my all, even when it sucks. And if you truly know me, you know I think and rethink everything over and over in my head. I am a doer, but I do walk through the process over and over in my head. I eventually remind myself that no change will be made until I make that step, even if it is not laid out perfectly.

So this conversation with my cousin made me realize I was getting my second chance and that meant I would not settle, so on day six, I quit. Why waste my time? I would find another way, which then led me to selling leggings. I still have in-studio clients that refer to me as "the legging lady" as it is how they first met me.

Then I went on to start an online auction business with two other people, which taught me many things, such as if you are going to run your own business, you better LOVE it because the hours you need to give it are endless. I hated the auction world. So here I was again at a crossroads . . .

One day when the kids went to school, I went downstairs, and I can't remember why but I felt defeated. I couldn't find my passion or my purpose. I lay on the floor and stared at the ceiling. I felt so lost and so empty in that moment, like I was an empty shell. Then my phone rang. Normally, I wouldn't answer when I felt like that, but it was my cousin, the same one who I wrote about earlier, and he had been going through divorce at this time too.

I answered, and he asked what I was doing. I said, "I am just laying here, Cor, staring at the ceiling." The words he said next will be stuck in my head forever. He said, "That's okay, Jo, just don't stay there!" There was so much comfort and power in that sentence. I think about it often. When things are hard, it is just a moment, and even if it has knocked me on my ass, I will sit and cry, then think, *Okay, Jo, pull it together and get back up!* We talked further on the phone, and I confessed to him, "When I wake up in the morning, I feel like throwing up, and before I close my eyes before going to bed at night, I feel the same way." It was like a constant state of anxiety. He said he felt the same way. I guess I felt comfort in knowing I was not alone or losing my mind. I said, "I wonder if that will ever leave?" I can't tell you when it left, it just did, and I do remember later saying, "Cory, I don't know when it left, but it has." The journey through the tunnel was happening.

Life with Corvel

Corvel was an idea from a friend in Kelowna. She said, "Name your favourite wine glass. Then you always have a date, you never are alone, and a wine glass never talks back or hurts you." I picked the name Corvel from the announcer whom I saw from a distance at my first Tough Mudder. The Tough Mudder is a nineteen-kilometre obstacle course that challenges your physical and your mental grit. He was a handsome man with muscles. Oh, need I go on?! And so, in the summer of 2014, often every other weekend when my kids were not at home, I dated Corvel. He was trustworthy. He showed up and never left, and one summer, he was my habit.

The thing about Corvel is the day after he visited, he would make my emotions bigger. My sadness would become larger than life. I refer to it as my "drinking blues," where you drink to numb the pain only to find your pain is tenfold the next day. This is how I managed one summer, if you want to call it managing.

I saw many divorced people go down the road of reliving it all. I told my mom that I had no use for it, then I realized I was doing the exact same thing, except I was classy because I had named my wine glass … not! I was always aware of what booze could do, as I come from a line of alcoholics. Drinking had scared me as a child, yet I had gone on to party hard, but I was always checking myself. I say this a lot, but training saved me: saved my heart and saved me from falling completely in love with Corvel and that vicious cycle. I do not ever say this statement lightly: I liked who I was when I lifted weights. I felt strong and capable. After a date night with Corvel, I felt afraid, broken, and so alone.

That summer as I dated Corvel, I was swinging kettlebells and hanging out more and more with this new kettlebell crew. They fascinated me, a crew who would get together on the weekends to watch fights and not drink. It was foreign to me to attend functions and not have drinking alcohol be a part of the event. I always thought that society expected this to be the norm. What I was beginning to understand is that we get to find and create our own norms. I was turning a corner, and my lifestyle was changing. I realized I could be whoever I needed to be. I was beginning to connect with what made me feel good about myself.

In preparation for my first official photo shoot that summer, I decided to take photos beforehand, and then stop drinking for four weeks. If I wanted, I had vodka with water, a splash of cranberry juice, and a lime wedge, in a glass which I did not name. I was in pretty good shape at the time, but when I looked at the photos afterward, I could not believe the difference that sobriety had made on my body. Not taking on the fog, I had become even more muscularly defined for the first time. I could, and I would, change my lifestyle. I would break up with Corvel and start dating LIFE!

Child Support

During the pandemic, my business struggled just as other businesses did. It was a big challenge. I have lived minimally, although on social media, it may seem that the opposite is true. Our world is confused, or at least I believe the humans within it are. I work very hard to help people in a good honest way, but being on social media has exposed me to people who have a strong preference for wanting to purchase particular pictures for themselves.

In twenty minutes, when funds were tight, I made $200 for pictures of my feet. I joke because I literally used the money to pay child support to my ex, who could easily take all of the family to various hot holidays and ski trips, while I was struggling to build my company and buying groceries made my stomach turn. I was happy he could take them, I just wished I could do the same. So the pictures were of the soles of my feet. It was so incredibly bizarre! To make $200 as a trainer, I would have had to put in two and a half hours of work. In twenty minutes, I had that $200 in my bank account.

How did I feel? Well, the photos were not dirty, but I felt odd, like I had sold a bit of my soul. I did talk to my daughters about this. I had a conversation with them about doing what feels good in your soul and letting their internal compasses navigate them.

Baggage

Our past should never define us, but it is part of us. I take all my lessons and experiences with love, even the super hard ones. I do not wish they didn't happen, I simply welcome them in as part of what molded me. I do not walk through my day as the bitter ex-wife of a bad divorce. I use those experiences to understand what pain and uncertainty does, and I take it forward as it has made me stand in my power, time and time again. Though parts of me will not understand certain things, I recognize that maybe I am not always suppose to understand all things.

I believe we "think" we need to carry our baggage from the past like a badge of honour, slugging it through our stories or situations, but this is not the case. I think the beauty of it all is that we can take off that backpack of baggage, put it down, thank it for its lessons, and leave it behind. So many beautiful people I talk with are carrying pain when I truly think they carry it as a punishment as they unknowingly think they deserve it. I did that a lot over the years. I do believe that we get used to being in the shit, embracing it so fully that it takes on a life of its own. It becomes our comfort zone. We become survivors, and we are good at it.

I was very good at it, until one day when I decided I didn't want to survive anymore. I want to thrive, and I want to walk through life serving others with love. My journey brought me here not to hurt continuously but to shine light on hard situations because there is always a lesson and a reason to let light in. Every morning when I wake up, I thank the universe for allowing me another day to bring the best I can to this incredible place.

CHAPTER 6:

VISIONARY

Did You Know?

At a young age, I discovered how great it was to move. Did you know that when you exercise, your muscles secrete proteins called myokines into your bloodstream? These are great for your brain health because they make you resilient to stress and can protect you from depression. Myokines are nicknamed "hope molecules."

Not really knowing the science behind it as a young child, I just connected with the fact that exercise made me feel better! When I was stressed, I would run, sometimes far away, until I got hungry and had to go home. I carried this strategy forward without even realizing it, until I looked back and started to connect the dots.

In the early morning before my young kids got up, swimming gave me hope that I could be the superhero mom and wife. And when my kids went to school, I would train endlessly, as internally I was fighting with my unhappiness. Until that day I faced myself in the mirror. Training has taught me many things. I used it to survive my divorce, my internal demons, and ultimately to navigate my business and my personal work, as it relates and reflects everywhere.

Embracing physical exercise was important to me. As I navigated my training, I enrolled my girls also into Muay Thai. I would get them up early Saturday morning—like I had to be a Muay Thai at 8:00 a.m. Now, let me tell you, in Saskatchewan, 8:00 a.m. in the middle of winter is not pleasant. They would come with me, but not be overly happy about it. I would train, then they would train in the kids' program. I remember like it was yesterday; after one class was coming out, we started throwing snowballs at each other. We got into the vehicle, and Mira looked at me with her rosy cheeks and said, "Isn't it amazing how grouchy we are in the morning, then how great we feel after training?!" I knew then that implementing this habit and them connecting that within themselves would be life-changing.

There was a time when I had no idea that training was going to be a huge part of my life, yet it came to encompass my life and my business.

The Life-Changing Decision

In December 2016, I decided to get certified in kettlebell at the place I was currently training. I would go work on my certification at 5:00 a.m., and then train again at 6:00 a.m. with everyone like normal. It was one of my steps in learning many things.

After I was certified, I decided to teach some classes near my place. It was a hard transition for me, as the 6:00 a.m. family I had found did not express excitement for me as I had hoped. They were my training friends, my family, and as I went out on my own, I felt those familiar feelings of being alone. I was learning that my inner happiness and decisions should never be created by anyone other than myself. I was learning a lot about life through experiences and training.

After continuing to teach and train with my 6:00 a.m. family, we had shot four hours of video the day before I had hurt my back. I laid on the couch thinking, *I found what I love, and here I am, laid out injured.* I did the four-hour shoot but started to research more training courses to level up my kettlebell training.

I had started training in Muay Thai after my best friend Holly asked me to try something new. I had also wanted to be able to defend myself, as I am just under five foot four inches tall, and I am 116 lb. soaking wet, so Muay Thai was good for self-defence. And what an incredible stress reliever. With the kettlebell training and the Muay Thai training, I eventually found Kettlebell Kickboxing, a martial arts training academy in NYC.

Kettlebell Kickboxing had a certification program that fused kettlebell and martial arts together. I found it on Instagram and fell in love with the idea, maybe a little bit too much in love as I was business GREEN!! Anyway, I reached out to the owner, Dasha Libin Anderson, who told me to fly down to be certified. I was the easiest person to market to. The difference here was I had also pitched my abilities to coach and teach. I wanted to work for her and certify trainers in Canada. She replied back saying we could have a meeting when I was there. I was going to do this!!

Some of my family and friends thought I was having a midlife crisis, and maybe I was because I DID NOT WANT TO WASTE MY LIFE! I remember having Starbucks with my mom and daughter Mira. I told my mom what I was going to do, and she blatantly looked at me and said, "No, you are not!" My daughter's eyes darted at me, and I simply replied, "I am going to NYC, and I am going to get her to hire me." Then I got up to take a walk amongst the books in Chapters. My daughter followed along closely, and when we got down one of the aisles, she stopped me by grabbing both my hands. She looked up at me and said, "Mom, I am so proud of you for going after what you want!" I don't know if she felt that way later, but in that moment, I remember thinking, *Your children are watching, so show them what you can do at forty. Show them that you are capable so they learn that they are capable too.*

I flew to NYC in March of 2017. I chose to go alone because I wanted to be uncomfortable, and I wanted nobody holding my hand. I was strong and capable, even though I was scared. I had never travelled out of the country alone before, and I was going to spend six days in a hotel in NYC. My mom had offered to come, but I had wanted to do it alone. I was nervous, but I had a sense that I was on the right path. If we allow ourselves to listen, we will hear the whisper that tells us we are doing the right thing. I was ready for this adventure, but even if I wasn't ready, it was too late now to back out! Ready, set, go!

For six days in NYC, I trained martial arts for up to five hours per day. This was on top of my Level 1 KBIA Certification and my Level 2 KBIA Master Level Certification. After day one, Dasha agreed to hire me to work for her. I was over the moon! I then taught my first class of thirty clients, as when she'd asked me if I would like to, the word yes had slipped out of my mouth before I even realized it.

My mindset was changing. I was tired of worrying and being scared. I wanted to LIVE and experience life. I was no longer going to sit in the stands of my own life. I wanted not to just participate in it, I wanted to LEAD it!

I would go on to take in my first NBA game while I was there. I took the subway alone and watched the game alone. Honestly, I wanted to take a cab, but when I went downstairs to the lobby, the front desk lady said, "Honey, you ain't taking a cab. You will never make it on time." She drew me a map and promised, "You got this, girl."

At the game, a woman beside me leaned over halfway through and said, "You must really like b-ball to come alone!" I would not be afraid of doing things alone. This trip was all about being out of my comfort zone. Each night, I would fall back into bed exhausted but laughing out loud at this crazy adventure I was living!

When I got back home, I almost immediately found two trainers to certify. As I was navigating my newfound passion and purpose, I was still trying to function in this new schedule of rotating weeks with my children, as I was referred to by my ex as a "part-time parent." Though I knew I had found what lit the fire inside me, I felt the sense that people regarded me as a dreamer. It was once recommended that I be a Walmart greeter, not really my dream job, but I feel like I would have crushed that job. I was trying to navigate through life and the changes that I had set in motion.

Sometimes, when it got hard, I would beat myself up and say, "Jodi, you picked this path, so deal with it." I would have to learn to be kinder to myself. My relationship with my ex had scaled to toxic. I went through feeling confused about how you could love someone at one time and have three children together, yet not be able to find common ground together and navigate life. Today, I have a different perspective on what love really is; I have had a relationship with another man that did not work out, yet we still can talk and find loving kindness between us. I know hurt people hurt people, so I was taking the brunt of the hurt.

Being told to get a man because I wouldn't make it on my own stung. Did you know that according to a *Harvard Business Review* study (Zenger and Folkman 2013), it takes an average of nearly six positive comments to counteract one negative comment made toward us? I was no stranger to how words hurt, and how they haunted. I honestly would rather be sucker punched, as I would carry negative words so far into my life. So far that I would refuse to let any man get close to me, so I could avoid falling into the trap of ever depending on someone again. I would have to learn to find harmony or risk being alone and feeling negatively toward men all my life. I had lots of work to do. I promised myself I would feel the weight of the words and then remove the power behind the words, and I was working through my newfound internal dialogue.

I planned on another trip back to NYC for more training. Three days before I left, I got a call from Dasha. She offered me an opportunity to buy up the Canadian region and wanted me to think about it before I arrived. "OH MY GOD!" I screamed after I got off the phone. My girls, who were in the kitchen with me at the time, looked at me like I was crazy! I couldn't believe the opportunity, and I was not sure how I would ever pull it off. I remember thinking, *I have no freaking clue how I am going to do it, but I am going to do it!!* I just needed a plan.

So I boarded the plane with a different plan, but I knew one thing would roll into another. I giggle now looking back at how green I was. At the time, I was a forty-one-year-old woman flying to NYC to try to figure out how I was going to buy the Canadian freaking region.

I lay in bed in my hotel in SoHo, crunching numbers and thinking about investors. Not just any investors. I needed people who could visualize what we could do and where we could go with our company. When I returned back home, I realized that since I was already in the process of selling my home, I would use that money, but that would take a bit. I had to talk to my parents and tell them what I was doing, as I was going to have to ask for help.

Asking for Help

The day went like this: When we went down to visit, my dad was finally coming to terms with me being divorced, but then I told him I was starting my own company and needed help funding it while my house was sold. I remember it like it was yesterday. The weather was beautiful. The kids were inside with Granny. I was sitting outside with Dad, and our conversation started getting heated. Remember the soft-spoken person I used to be? Well, no longer. I told him that with or without his help and support, I was going to find a way to do it. I even pointed my finger at him (a sign I am surely mad when I need to make a point). He bluntly said to me, "Doesn't matter what I say to you, you are going to fucking do what you want!" I agreed and walked into the house, my heart pounding so hard. I hate confrontation, and standing up to my dad was huge for me.

When I drove home, I remember feeling proud of myself for standing up for what I believed in and voicing my opinion. I was taking the leap of faith to do exactly what I wanted. It was the first time I recognized that if you can feel pride inside for yourself, nobody can ever touch that. It is untouchable if you can create it within yourself. It is like when you finally realize that lifting kettlebells allows you a confidence inside that is secretly yours. You do not need a pat on the back because you created it within, so you can pat yourself on the back. This was a moment I will cherish forever, even though it was a hard and heated conversation. I talked to my kids about the importance of feeling proud of yourself and your accomplishments without always trying to gain that from another person. Today, my kids call these talks "Mom's philosophical moments."

The Launch

My parents had agreed to help with funding until I could sell my house. I had one more trip to NYC, and then I could organize the launch of the Canadian region. In seven days, I met the infamous Steve Maxwell and got a private certification with him. I then was learning how to navigate my website. I was pleasantly surprised to know the site was run by WordPress, as I was familiar with it because of my online business, which I don't believe was a coincidence. I was always learning. My first big business and life lesson was learning to enjoy the journey.

The day I launched KBKB Canada, I was so excited, but the day was like a grand letdown. Reflecting back, I focus on the journey that got me to that day in October 2017! The business model was to certify trainers across Canada. Seeing where we are today, six years later, I am reminded that the journey is what's important because sometimes the end goals just keep changing and evolving.

CHAPTER 7:

QOP

You might ask, "What is QOP?" For me, it is my circle of great humans whom I know are healthy and productive in this life. I think to live a full, great, abundant life, you need QOP (Quality-Only People).

We often get confused with thinking family is part of this. Some of us are fortunate to have family who are supportive, while others have to learn to let go of family if they are toxic. Toxic people are toxic—blood relation or not. I have seen people struggle to engage with their family, justifying it by simply saying, "They are family!" I think family are the people who love you and allow you to grow. Family should add support, not take it away. Family can be found anywhere. For me, some of my closest "family members" were found at a Muay Thai gym and later in my kettlebell world.

As I was growing my business and struggling, I learned from a close friend that I should spend less time with people who drained me because I was in the business of filling up cups. I needed my downtime to be with people who wanted to fill my cup. These QOP will know what your silence means; they will hold space for you and help remind you that they believe in you on the days you falter. On one of my hardest days, one of my QOP said, "You just do you. That's more than enough." These are the types of people you want in your corner. These are your people!

$40 in Lindt Chocolates

I hope you all have that one best friend, the one who knows all your secrets and still loves you anyways!

I have this friend, and I will tell you that if I had not gotten married, I likely would have never met her. When I got separated, my ex went to her and asked her to pick between us, as really she had been his friend first. She is the type of person who would never think to pick between two people; it is simply not who she is, but after that day, she picked me. I tease that I won her in the divorce. If you are divorced, you will understand this. Friends you think you had are no longer your friends. Neighbours whom you sat with around the fire on summer nights no longer talk with you, yet they holiday with your ex.

When I was going through really hard shit, she would sit in a parking lot with me, and we'd both bare our souls. I can't count how many times we cried in the Costco parking lot, Starbucks too.

One day, we thought screw it and went and spent $40 on Lindt chocolates. We cried, or at least I cried, ate chocolate, and drank coffee. I hope you never have to experience this pain, but if you do, I hope you have a friend like this in your hard times—whether you both are hot messes or maybe just one of you and the other sits there in silence while snot runs down your face. These friends are your lifetime friends. You don't need them in your space 24/7, but you'll drive to their home where you can sit, have coffee, and connect like you just saw each other yesterday. She is forever my soul sister because she knows too much!!

Trip to Calgary

My first flight I took to Calgary after my separation turned out to be the first time I had to take a cab alone. No joke, I had not navigated life alone EVER. Seems incredibly bizarre to me now. I remember riding in the cab to my friend's house, and I was staring outside the window like I was seeing life for the first time. Maybe I was seeing it for the first time. I was chatting with the cabbie. Oh yes, I was excited. I was excited to discover myself and this world around me. When I got to my friend's house, I thanked the cabbie over and over.

When I entered my friend's house, I was so excited to tell her that I had made it, like I thought I was going to get lost or abducted! I had successfully navigated from the airport to her house, and I can honestly feel the joy inside me right now as I had felt it that day! She was so kind, smiling and telling me, "Good job!" She was like the eager parent who listens to her kindergartener's first day at school! I was elated. I think it was when my sense of wonder started to grow. I giggle thinking about the girl in that cab, so ready to experience life.

I feel it is important to share a special note about the people you surround yourself with. Have people around you who love and support you, and if they can't, then you have to spend less time with the people who don't support you.

True Intentions

Along my journey, I have had friends stay and friends go. I found I became so focused on my journey that some friends drifted away. On retreats, I will tell my clients working on mindset to make sure their intentions come from a pure heart. Their intention may still be misinterpreted, but they have no control over another person's perspective.

I had an experience with a friend … I reached out to them to wish them a happy birthday. I wrote, *Happy Birthday. Love, Jodi.* The reply back was: *I used to have a friend named Jodi long ago.* They then went on to say our friendship was not a priority in my life. I've learned that when someone makes a comment like this, it is not a me thing but likely something going on with them. I hold no anger, but I share this because I felt sadness for a person whom I only wished happy birthday and whom I have incredible memories with.

As I grow this business, I realize if I am going to continue to level up, I have to make sacrifices. Unfortunately, this can turn out to be sacrificing some relationships along the way. They do say entrepreneurship is a lonely path, and I understand that now more than ever. Nobody is meant to share your dreams, so they can't be expected to understand your ways.

Looking back, the summer that friendship drifted, I recall they were busy with a new relationship, which was great, and I was happy for them. It was also the summer when all my children moved out of my home, and I had to find a more affordable home fast, like within a month, and I was awaiting abnormal test results. Remember life is not always as it seems; their perspective was that I let our friendship fall away, while all I remember was trying to breathe and navigate my life. I had not meant to be hurtful, but I think most of our intentions are not to hurt or cause pain. I never walk through this life with intentions to cause pain, but realizing my boundaries and taking care of myself does not always fit with everyone around me. I still go forward while cherishing my memories.

As we move forward, we often do not stay in the same circle. I find no sadness in this as I believe your people will always be your people, but sometimes friendships are like seasons, and if you grow, not everyone will grow with you. Growth involves change, so do not stay in one place because you are afraid to lose friends. Your Quality-Only People will understand, or at least they will stand in your space and be there. I have friends whom I have not seen in years, and yet we can embrace in a hug and catch up over coffee like we haven't missed a beat. I wish no ill will on anyone. Life ebbs and flows. Carrying hurt and pain is a choice, and I choose to let the light in and walk through this life with good intentions.

Men and Dating after Marriage

I love men, I lust them, and I hate them all at once. People over the years ask me a lot, "Are you dating? Will you get remarried?" You know, people are curious. I will share with you a bit about my personality toward men and my drive for my own success.

When I was a teen, I lived in a small community, and I wanted out. My friends were having sex, and some of my friends got pregnant. So I decided I would not have sex because I wanted out, and that was an odds game I would not play. I watched not only friends but grown married women live under the thumb of the men who supposedly loved them. So at a young age, I was strict with a lot of things. I dated, but those were mostly short relationships because teenage boys want sex. I was called a tease and dumped lots of times, and you know what, at times it really sucked, but at the end of the day, I wouldn't change it.

My ex was my first partner, and that was not until I had almost graduated from university. I speak very frankly to my children about sex, as I think it is so important to talk, and not surface talk but real talk. I talk about not being afraid of one's sexuality and that being sexual is great, but also to remember the related risks. I am not as fearful. I think sex is great, and I think making love is great. I was a kid who knew at the time that she didn't want to get "stuck." I have learned so much about love and sex and how you should have both in a partner. I didn't used to know the difference. I had thought that when you had a partner, it was always love, but it's not. So my career in business took the front of my life.

I fell madly in love after I separated from my ex. This relationship rocked my world. I found someone to fill a void in me. Yes, I know you are thinking that I used him to fill a void. I decided to build big, strong, concrete walls because I didn't think I could manage the heartache with the heavy burden of a new company, a hellish divorce, and feeling disconnected from my children. So I built big walls. I had built so many walls I don't think we stood a chance at surviving. I never trusted love and never trusted us, and if you don't have trust, you don't have a foundation to build on.

He taught me many things. He was a gift to me, and I will be forever grateful for our time together and our friendship. He reminds me that not all relationships have to end in complete turmoil. It actually allowed me to have a conversation with my daughter, who was afraid to date because of potential breakups. Remember, she watched her parents, and we were the best example of an explosion with casualties. I told her that not all relationships end that way, and if you truly love each other, you can walk away and keep some of that love intact.

I know it was a long time ago, but I was so hurt and saddened when he broke things off. However, when you learn from your experiences, you no longer look back at them as painful but in gratitude because every experience teaches us. There were all these moments with him that made me happy, and this is key in relationships.

You need someone to add to your already existing happiness, which comes from within. I no longer look for someone to fill my cup, as I can do that myself. I make myself happy. Life taught me how to fall in love with myself. It is the most beautiful and fulfilling experience. It brings you peace, like so much that I really do have a hard time articulating it.

Social media talks smack, like "love yourself, love your body." It's not really smack, but if you ever reach that place, you will be in awe of it. When you accomplish things and it becomes so internal, you will have little concern for what the outside world thinks. I needed this heartache in order to learn. It smacked me upside the head with the knowledge that I want to be whole so that when I find the right person to take a chance on, I will go into that relationship without fear. I will be excited in knowing I bring a whole person to the table, not a person who is needing to fill in the void.

My current thoughts on men are that I have goals and dreams that take me to other places. I do not want to get stuck or stay somewhere when I have no guarantees, so I've gone back to my high school mentality.

Yes, I still will have sex, but I will not get into a relationship now. Unless I get blindsided, I am focusing on me, my kids, my business, and where I want to be in the next three years. There has been someone I have talked to for years, and yet we have never been able to connect. I don't know if this person has been placed in my life as a healthy distraction or if it is someone I will one day see. Only the universe knows. For now, I am good alone. I have learned to be strong alone. I miss physical touch, and I miss the other great things about relationships, but I will not just find a partner to fix those moments. I will never settle. My partner will be brilliant, smart, goal-oriented, and love me so much. He is just not ready yet, and maybe I am not yet either.

Rosie

I got my puppy, Rosie, in 2020, eleven days after I had opened the studio and during all the chaos. Then I had a major anxiety attack and called someone, saying, "You need to take her. I cannot be responsible for a pet." This is ironic because I had been responsible for a company, trainers, and a studio location—oh yeah, and three children! She said, "Just keep her for a week. It is very normal to feel like this." In the back of my mind, I was thinking, *Maybe the kids will come back home if I keep her because they were so excited to come with me to get her.* That didn't happen, but my youngest did stay with me more that summer, and she was Rosie's person!

Now, being the active person I was, I walked her three times a day. Sometimes, this poor little puppy would collapse on the grass and refuse to move. I was quite distant with her. I did what I needed to do with her and then went about my business in the studio and worked on my court case. Yet I began enjoying our outdoor walks as it connected me back to nature.

People would always want to pet Rosie, so it was so nice seeing others smile. Little by little, this fury, four-legged creature was sneaking her way into my heart. I hadn't loved or allowed anyone to get close to me, and then one morning, I said out loud, "You little shit, I think I love you." She came into my life at the time I felt it was the worst. Turns out, she came at the right time, just like the universe does. I had always heard how animals help us to heal, but I'd never really understood it until Rosie. Slowly, I was healing, and 2020 was the hardest year again, but also a year of major learning and evolving. Since having Rosie, I have apologized to my son for not letting him have a cat when he was hurting from the divorce. I was wrong not to let him have a furry friend to love and connect with.

My Adventurous Mama Bear

I cannot write this book and not write about my mom. I can hardly write those words without tears welling up in my eyes. I love her as my mom but also as my best friend in the entire universe. Our relationship has always been unique, and when I was younger, there were times when I wished things were different between us. I no longer think that way or wish that.

She has taught me so much about character. We all pick our path, and at times I wished she had picked differently, but I value all she has chosen. At the end of the day, I love the strength and the unity she holds within our family unit. When I look at my mom, I see her strength and her courage to do what she could with what life handed her.

We have worked through a lot. She has always been there for me to hold my hand. She didn't fight me on my decision to leave my marriage, and she held space for me always. When my first real relationship ended after my marriage, she laid there beside me, holding my hands as I sobbed myself to sleep. She has a story that tells of her strength, though it is her story to tell, not mine. She has brought so much laughter and light into my life and my children's.

We have often taken girls' trips, but one in particular stands out. It was a trip to the mountains. We had stopped by Starbucks to get drinks before our kayaking adventure. We got in the car, and my mom looked at me with such excitement and said, "Isn't that great they just give out free water in that basket?" My girls' eyes got huge. I told Mom that water was not free. She said, "Well, you got three." I added, "Yes, I know, but I also paid for three!" The adventure was beginning.

We got to the place where we could go kayaking, but my mom declined coming and said there was no need to rent a kayak for her. So me and the girls headed out as Granny—which we all call her—was going to sit and read on the beach.

While we were pointed away from the beach, I heard my name being called. I looked back over my shoulder to see my mom beelining straight toward us in a streamline-looking kayak. The girls giggled. "Oh no, Granny stole a kayak!" Turns out, she had been chatting it up with the lady on the beach, telling her that her daughter and granddaughters were out kayaking. The lady had given her a luxurious kayak and sent her out to us.

It is my mom's way to connect with people. She is sometimes naive to the ways of the world but always moving through life with a big heart. When someone ever says that I am just like my mom, it is the greatest feeling inside. And in this moment, as I know she will read this in print, I need to say: I love you, Mom. Your sacrifices never went unnoticed, and your anchor has kept us all together when the waves were so incredibly rocky!

No shame and no regrets, just life and the never-ending challenge of trying to navigate it with love.

CHAPTER 8:

RESILIENCY

Waterfall Story

My first fitness retreat was in January 2020. I took some clients to Jamaica with a Zumba crew! On the first day, one of my clients, Iva, slipped on concrete, hit a lounge chair, and dislocated her toe. She came over to me and said, "Jodi, look at my baby toe." I looked down, and it was pointing out. I looked at her as she seemed to be not in pain, and said, "Does it always look like that?" I was thinking, *Oh my God, we are in a foreign country.*

The front desk wanted to send an ambulance. Iva is tough like nobody else I have ever met besides my mom, and I knew she did not need any ambulance. We lined up a driver to take us to the nearest local hospital, but I had also messaged a friend who was a nurse. She texted, *Just YouTube on how to reset it.* The thought made me want to puke, but regardless, we all watched the YouTube video on how to reset the toe.

So picture this: Iva, me, Sean (another one of my trainers), and our personal driver, Rocky. He said it would likely take us twelve hours to get this sorted, including the drive, the hospital admittance, and the procedure.

I realized I needed a charger for my phone, which gave us time to think as Rocky got out to find a charger for me. I looked at Iva and Sean, and it was like we all had the same thought: *Should we try resetting it? Twelve hours of our holiday will be shot otherwise!* Iva said, "Yeah, let's!" I looked at Sean, silently communicating, "Please tell me you can do this." I offered to hold Iva's hand to distract her. Rocky said, "You Canadians are nuts!" Sean got out, Iva looked at me, and I held her hand. I said something, but I'm not sure what, and we heard a pop sound. I thought, *Ta-da, reset.* We were laughing as we taped Iva's toe, got her a bag of ice, and sat her up on a lounge chair with strict instructions to sit!

The following day, we had booked a waterfall climb, and not just a little one but a 900-foot climb. I had trained and had known Iva for a while at that point. I knew she was a resilient woman, and I knew she had already accomplished so much she had wanted to try, so I knew she would overcome on that day too. This story gives me goosebumps because I equally have learned so much as I walk along the fitness journeys of my clients.

That day, I stood at the bottom of the fall with my determined client, who had dislocated her toe only the day before, and I knew it was sore. She didn't say so, but I knew. I stood there, looking at her and then looking all the way up. There were slippery rocks every step of the way. I had a moment of thinking, *Oh my God, how am I going to help get her to the top??*

Then life experience and my training set in as quick as the moment of uncertainty. One step. Each section had a platform level, so we would accomplish one level at a time. We also had a guide who was incredible. So level by level, we made the climb, and each section was celebrated. It was one of the most incredible moments I'd had so far with Iva. The photos we took showed such happiness on our faces.

Life is exactly like that waterfall climb. We get overwhelmed by the big goal that is ahead, but when we break it down and enjoy the journey, the journey becomes as much of the success as the final destination point. I am grateful to walk alongside Iva and see her determination.

I also had the honour of having her join and complete her first Spartan Race in the summer of 2022, at the age of seventy-four! We reached the top of the last climb, and then I sat and massaged out her calves as they were cramping so bad, but she finished!

I love this woman. She is my *kokum* ("grandmother" in Cree, and I am her *nosisim*, "granddaughter"). We adopted each other on our first fitness retreat, and we are kindred spirits who have lived hard but know that our mindset is strong, and we are stronger together.

Perspective

Our perspective is molded from our experiences. I want to share a story about Covid. I invited my children to Easter dinner. They did not come out of fear. They feared that I was possibly unsafe because of my perspective on Covid. When you look at things, use your intellect first to gather information, but then remember people's experiences will reflect their actions. For this particular event, I cooked a ham dinner. Out of fear, they did not attend, as they knew I was still going for walks with other people during the lockdown. Though they did order sushi with their dad and have it delivered. I thought, *Strangers prepping their meal and delivering it?*

I also learned something else: When you survive a traumatic experience, it lessens your fear. I found my fear was lessened because I had gone through different trauma than my ex and my children. So I could stand back and be less fearful.

Another example of this is when I did the twenty-one-day virtual challenge with the ex-Navy SEAL, and I didn't finish because my doctor asked me to take a day to heal and rest. When we did our meeting, Thom said, "So you chose to listen to a doctor? You could have broken them up to finish the exercises." He was not wrong. He was a man who had been in battle, where if you broke something, a doctor may tell you not to move that body part, but you moved for survival. He had different trauma and experiences, so a small procedure was minor. Different experiences should never diminish yours, but it is important to understand and stand back and look at the big picture. I am always aware that we all see through different lenses depending on our life experiences!

Never Let Fear Stop You

I was invited to do mobility training by my online training client, who ironically is another ex-Navy SEAL. His organization, The Stand Up Veterans Foundation (SUP Vets), is a nonprofit organization that promotes teaching veterans and active duty military the soothing power of the ocean and the joy of standup surfing. He invited me down to Mexico to teach mobility to the members before they surfed. Now with any experience, whether I am doing a certification or teaching a class, I am always open to learning from others. I think we can always learn from each other, even when we are teaching.

I want to share an experience I had on this particular trip. As you know, I live in Saskatchewan, and it is a landlocked province, so the ocean looks really, really big to a prairie girl. I was learning through experience how to navigate going on a retreat where I knew that in order to be accepted, I would have to be brave enough to take on the waves.

I went into the trip knowing this: I am physically strong and also mentally strong, but strength does not mean the absence of fear. Looking at the ocean reminds me of how I feel when I travel to the Canadian Rockies and look up at the mountains ... simply SMALL.

The night before everyone arrived, the vets spoke of the ocean as having a heartbeat of its own, which you feel when you surf. They went on to tell stories of sharks, jellyfish, and sharp rocks. I kept on smiling, but inside I was shitting my pants, thinking, *Why didn't I go swimming and practice?* It had been so long since I had swum. The other factor was being around ex-Navy SEALS, air aviators, and coast guards, all of whom work to protect and are so incredibly brave. I was going to do it no matter what. I would embrace the uncomfortable and hold comfort in the fact that if I started drowning, I would have a great team around me!

Day one was great. They put me in "the penalty box," as they called it. The waters there were safe for practice. Our organization had two world-champion surfers with us, so we were taught by the best. In calm waters, I knew I was more than capable.

On day two, a Navy SEAL asked if I was going on today. I smiled and said, "Sounds like a plan" or something that held no maybes. Then the instructor asked me, "Are you ready?" He only asked because he needed me to say yes. I looked at him and said, "I know I am strong enough, but I need you to teach me how to go into the ocean and how to get back out." I needed two things: guidance on my journey and knowing how to get out when I was ready. It was kind of like how I navigate people to start their training and how to progress or modify as they need.

He showed me an entry. We had to try again because I walked with the board on the wrong side of me. There were three ways: stand by the board and guide it over the smaller waves, give it a push away and dive under, or jump on and go over the wave. I was freaking out inside, but I trusted in him and the process. I also trusted that God had not brought me that far to have me hurt or die in this ocean. Fear would not win, but my faith would. The second try, we dove down, then jumped on and paddled like there was no tomorrow. He got out to where the waves dissipated and you could float. Smiling, he looked at me and said, "You made it! How was it?" I said, "Not going to lie, I was actually scared shitless, but I made it!"

Fear does not go away, and situations do not go away either, but how we deal with them and within them is key. I will always ask myself, *If I do not do this, will I regret it?* And then I allow my faith to be bigger than my fear. Truthfully, both are unknown, but the positive energy lives within faith.

When I practiced my exit from the ocean that day, the biggest wave of the day decided to join me, and I got tossed like a rag doll. I didn't drown or get hurt, but I did get left with a story to share. The joke on the retreat was: If you are looking for a big wave, stick near Jodi because they seem to like her!

Lesson of a Goose

I will leave you, my readers, with one final story that is both funny and invigorating!

As you may or may not know, when Canadian geese nest, they are vicious. They are nicknamed "cobra geese" because they are mean.

On my morning walks, I would avoid one area that was populated with Canadian geese because they scared me. Yes, I was scared, a grown woman walking with her dog, Rosie, who is half pit bull and half lab.

One day, when I was walking with my best friend Jacquie, we looked over our shoulders, and a Canadian goose was dive-bombing me. Literally, I screamed. I thought, *I have to run!* Yet, I was not able to run. I had to face this goose. I felt this power in that moment to stand my ground. I realized that I had a ninety-pound dog. We charged back, and the goose momentarily backed off. This happened two more times until we made some space between us.

Later, as I sat at home, I thought about fear, how the only way to diminish it is to really face it. It is an incredible feeling, and I have felt it many times over the years. The only way to be strong and not let fear control your life is to face it straight on. No, you won't die. Will you feel your heartbeat fast? Yes, but maybe you won't be able to hear your heart beating as the trauma is real. However, what is even more real is your ability to stand up to your fear each and every day!

AFTERWORD

How does one finish the last chapter in a story they are still writing? I want to share my heartfelt thoughts with you. I have learned so much being on this Earth. I have learned that most people are kind, and the ones who are unkind are usually hurting from trauma. You do not have to tolerate their backlash, but you should recognize that they too have pain that exists. Understand that we all have different perspectives when going through the same event. Our experiences will mold how we handle and see the event. Our perspective might not be the correct one as it is simply our perspective, so be mindful that others carry different perspectives. Learn how to process and feel emotion, but try to not navigate from emotion, as navigating from emotion is messy. I simply mean that you shouldn't let your emotions react to situations. Instead, learn how to act in situations.

I used to wish I could write something so profound that it would bring about an aha moment in my reader so they could skip all the pain. But I think it's important to take the time to breathe, move, and invite the pain in to sit with you; don't let the pain destroy you, but let it teach you. I believe pain is part of our stories. Every moment builds us. Sometimes, it has to break us down first so we can learn. I believe every lesson will be repeated until we figure it out. Being aware is so important. I sit here writing this after reading through all the stories I chose to share. I cry and I laugh at my journey and my adventures. I feel the whole of it, but I have learned to not allow myself to be consumed by it all either.

The following are lessons I'd like to share:

- A broken heart doesn't mend itself.
  That takes time and work.
- Loving yourself means having boundaries and letting go.
- Treat your body as if it's the only one you'll get. (It is.)
- Pausing is hard, but it's important for the mind, body, and soul.
- We aren't meant to be alone, although time alone is important in small doses.
- Challenge your body and your thoughts daily.
- Don't walk through this life thinking you are incapable. Walk through life asking the question, "Why not me?" Then get to work.
- Discipline and consistency is KEY.
- Surround yourself with QOP (Quality-Only People). You will need them.

REFERENCES

Singer, Michael A. 2013. *The Untethered Soul: The Journey Beyond Yourself.* Oakland, CA: Noetic Books, Institute of Noetic Sciences.

Zenger, Jack, and Joseph Folkman. 2013. "The Ideal Praise-To-Criticism Ratio." *Harvard Business Review*. https://hbr.org/2013/03/the-ideal-praise-to-criticism.

ABOUT THE AUTHOR

Jodi Barrett is a spirited woman with a fire in her soul and a love for coffee and M&M's! When life threw her punches, she stayed in the ring, determined to prove to herself that she could do anything and show her children that you can go after your dreams at any age. In her free time, Jodi enjoys writing, having adventures, swinging kettlebells, and spending time with her loved ones. She continues to motivate and inspire others to create a healthy lifestyle while embracing their oneness within.

She is residing in Regina, Saskatchewan until the wind blows her to the next landing spot.

She is a published writer for various wellness and fitness magazines across Canada and the United Kingdom. She co-authored *Sacred Hearts Rising: Sparks of Light*. This is her first memoir.

Printed in the USA
CPSIA information can be obtained
at www.ICGtesting.com
LVHW012113160124
769002LV00012B/892